The Good Detective's Guide To Library Research

How to Track the Elusive Fact

by Barbara J. Brown

Neal-Schuman Publishers, Inc.

New York   London

Published by Neal-Schuman Publishers, Inc.
100 Varick Street
New York, NY 10013

Printed and bound in the United States of America

Library of Congress Cataloging-in-Publication Data

Brown, Barbara J. (Barbara Jane)
    Good detective's guide to library research / by Barbara J. Brown.
      p. cm.
    Includes bibliographical references and index.
    ISBN 1-55570-197-3 (alk. paper)
    1. Libraries—United States.   2. Searching, Bibliographical.
  3. Information retrieval. I. Title.
Z710.B875 1995
025.5'24—dc20   95-30640

Contents

Introduction

The Keys to the Kingdom

Your teacher assigns you to write a report on dogs, the causes and effects of World War I, or the current trade deficit. Perhaps you volunteer to build a solar oven for a science project. Whatever the subject, the chances are you will probably do all or some of your research in a library. Library research can also help you get your vintage 1975 car functioning again, research the career you think you might like to pursue, locate some new programs for your computer, find material to uphold your side of the abortion debate, or see what courses different colleges offer.

As children, we wandered through the tall shelves of a neighborhood library, opening and closing books until we glimpsed another world so vivid the young reader was drawn right in, and the book checked out. Later, for that first research assignment, we tried to find what we needed in the old reliable way, pulling out books with titles that sounded relevant. Pleasant though that approach may be, navigation by browsing is not likely to satisfy serious research needs. Whether you're a student writing a term paper or a researcher investigating how to warp a loom, working your way through modern library configurations will offer the greatest rewards. That means that you will have to track down the information that you want.

How do you do that? How do you find and then use the

keys to this library kingdom? You have to learn to be a good detective. Like Sherlock Holmes, you must look beneath each stone, follow every lead, investigate all clues. But your task will be far easier than was Holmes's, provided that you learn to utilize and negotiate the systems in place to help you find your way.

This book is not intended to be a library science class, nor even to teach you to use this encyclopedia or that CD-ROM product. It is more like a wilderness survival course that helps you decide what track to follow, or what plants to eat, or what signs lead to water. This book will try to show you how to survive and thrive in a library. Any library. How to approach a problem, analyze it, and watch for the signs that will help you get to your answer.

For the most part, we will approach this from the perspective of a student, though the tips and techniques in this book will work whether you are a student working on a school assignment or John or Jane Q. Public trying to start a new business. While the major emphasis will be the public library and the school library, many of the same techniques may be used in college and university libraries.

Some people are stopped by a solid wall of books as soon as they enter a library and never get past that monolithic wall to the marvels that await them. Other people develop tunnel vision. They master a single path, scurry to the one small portion of the collection that houses their special interest, and never venture further. Worse still are those who view the library as a maze of confusing, book-lined alleys in which they will occasionally, by great serendipity, spot a treasure. But a library is a veritable kingdom of wonders, set up to function as a massive information retrieval system. Knowledge and understanding of the series of systems that constitutes the whole grants the lucky user the keys to this book-driven kingdom.

The information offered here is intended to serve as a basic guide to utilizing your library. Whether you are researching a school or a personal project, period costumes for a play, or the projected results of the greenhouse effect on agriculture, the ability to use the library is vital. Your library research may provide all you need, or it may serve as a springboard from which to do original research. Exciting new developments in library networks and electronic interactions permit even the cozy neighborhood libraries we browsed through as children to serve as entry points to extensive collections of information. A good part of the world's knowledge can be yours if you hone your skills as a sleuth. You will be limited only by your own desire to follow through. The possibilities can go on for a lifetime. Opportunities, information, and vast new worlds to be explored await you at your library.

Chapter One

Get That Information, Watson!
Being A Good Detective

L ibrary research requires good detective work. You
need to wring every last drop of knowledge from
your sources. Like a bloodhound, you follow the
scent of a possible lead. Each source can be a springboard
to another source. You, the diligent sleuth, track, trail, and
detect all the myriad bits of information that together reveal
the subject you are researching.

You must learn to follow tracks and clues through your
library and any other library you enter. The crucial starting
point is the most important source in your library: the librarian. A librarian knows his or her way through the maze of
computers, indexes, catalogs, handbooks and manuals that
may stand between you and The Answer. But librarians must
do a host of things in the library, and finding information
for you is only one of them. While cooperative librarians
may locate and follow the elusive trail to the information
you need, you will be better served if you learn to find it
yourself. Learning how to find information on your own will
ultimately be of far greater value to you than simply being
handed some easy answers.

Use the librarian as your guide, rather than jumping to the
deceptively easy path of asking him or her to get you the
information. An old proverb is apt here: be careful what you
wish for, lest you get it. Obtaining the answer without learn-

ing *how* it was derived will turn into a curse rather than a blessing. Sure it is tempting to approach a difficult assignment by phrasing it as a reference question to the librarian. Like magic, Ms. Jones or Mr. Smith pops up the information, and hands you the facts you need for the moment. But you will have no idea how to work your own way through the sources. The next time you need information you must go back to your helper and ask again. You also will not have garnered the valuable additional information you would have uncovered as an offshoot of the research process, had you done it on your own.

Be aware that while librarians can and will track down information for you in the form of reference questions, they cannot help you by doing hours of research. There are too many other people to help and too many other demands they must meet. This is just as well. If you are a student, part of a research project, undoubtedly the most important part, is learning to do the research yourself. Having someone else do it is self-defeating, since it prevents you from acquiring skills which you will need throughout your education and life.

Another factor to consider: you may need to retrace your steps. This may be difficult to imagine, but it happens *all* the time: you saw a bit of information in one of the many articles the librarian found for you, but you didn't mark it down because it didn't seem important at the time. Now it is absolutely vital! You can't live without it! Another scenario: you lost the three-by-five index card with bibliographic references to *the* key article backing up your arguments. If you don't find that article again you can't use that information. Unfortunately, Ms. Jones, the dedicated librarian who actually found those articles for you, has finally married Mr. Smith, and they are honeymooning in Paris. The other librarians are very helpful, but each seems to have a different search strategy. They have come up with almost everything you used and more, but not *the* source that Ms.

Smith found, that you now so desperately need.

Use librarians as guides and teachers. You will put in a little more time, but you will also know how a search was done, and how to do the next one. Most librarians are eager and enthusiastic teachers, and, like so many of us, they enjoy sharing their knowledge and expertise. It is part of their makeup to want to give you copies of the keys to the kingdom. In the best cases, it is part of their mission in life.

Be prepared when you go to the library. Assistance from librarians will work to your best advantage only if you first think out the specifics of what you really want. You should do this before you ask the librarian to show you how to find it. Does this sound ridiculously simple? It's not. People often ask for a related subject or for something they believe will lead them to what they want rather than asking for what they *really do* want. Define in your own mind exactly what you need to know, and ask for that. You and the librarian will be spared the wasted time and effort of answering the wrong question.

Be prepared to share information with the librarian that will help him or her to find exactly what you need. If you need something for a class, tell the librarian *what* class, the era you are studying, the subject area you are working on. Provide the point of view of your assignment, so the librarian understands how you will use the information. Suppose you ask how compact disks are made. Period. Your librarian reasonably starts to research the manufacturing process, thus launching a completely different search than what you really want to know: how you would go about cutting a demonstration disk of your new rock band.

Whether your subject is very obscure, like the Ciboney Indians, or very broad, like the history of the United States, explain specifically what you want. Then, and only then, your librarians will be able to help you locate whatever information is available in or through that library on your subject, as well as steer you to other, larger libraries as may be needed.

Let the librarians introduce you to all of the things they have available, including pathfinders, gazetteers, bibliographic databases, CD-ROM disks, and whatever else that library offers, but follow your own trail. You are the only one who can really tell if what you find is what you want and need. And now—on with the hunt!

Chapter Two

?

What Dewey Did, Does, and Might Do for You: How to Find One Book in a Million

How many books are in your local library? There are about 108,000 in mine. Even in a small library with a mere 25,000 to 30,000 volumes, how do you hone in on the one book or topic you need? The answer is exactly what Melvil Dewey figured out. Thomas Jefferson had figured it out before him. Each of these gifted men set up systems to arrange libraries so people could find the books they want. Dewey's system became the *Dewey Decimal Classification System*. You are probably familiar with it, as it is the system used in almost all public and school libraries. Mr. Jefferson's system evolved into the *Library of Congress Classification System*, commonly called LC. It is used mainly in college and university libraries, and, of course, the Library of Congress.

So, what's the best way to arrange a bunch of books? Many people line their shelves with books grouped neatly by size. They look attractive and it takes only a few minutes of hunting to find what you want. But that doesn't work very well for a few hundred books, and when you get up to a few thousand books you can forget about finding anything.

Perhaps you have the memory of a chess champion, and can put your hands on that special book within a minute. Okay, what happens when someone else uses those books? Or when hundreds or thousands of people use them, as in public and school libraries? Tom might think a particular book looks nicer in another location when he returns it, and Susie harbors a deep desire to cluster books by color. The books change places. They change places again as new books in a wide range of sizes and colors are added to the collection.

You might set up the library so that books are placed on the shelf in the same order in which they are purchased. The tenth book you buy is always the tenth book on the shelf and the 3,010th book you buy is always the 3,010th book on the shelf. Logical? Maybe. But it is almost as hard to find things as it is with the previous arrangement. In order for a library to make this system work they set up a card file or computer system that lets the user locate all the books on a subject. You can look something up and find out that there are books on dog training in 17th place and 133rd place and 1,769th place and—well, you get the idea.

Some libraries do use this system. They have what is called a "closed stack" system. That means that people never go to the shelves and browse, or look for their own books. Instead, they look through card files and then ask for the book they want. The librarian enters the stacks and brings out the book or books. In some highly automated libraries, a machine does the retrieving. This has not been a very popular system, though it has some advantages. The library keeps books in order and uses shelf space more effectively. Fewer books are stolen. But such a system is cumbersome, staff intensive, and not very user friendly. Those good old browsing days are eliminated completely.

What Thomas Jefferson and Melvil Dewey created were subject classification systems. These systems are used by most libraries in this country. That means that all books on dog training are together in one area. And books on ghosts, sports, cooking, and books on books, are shelved as a group rather than scattered randomly among thousands of other books.

The Dewey Decimal System, found in your neighborhood

or school library, uses numbers to arrange books into subject areas. The basic number always has three digits. For example, 796 refers to sports. A decimal and another set of digits are added on to further define the subject. Add .357, which refers to baseball, to the 796 that is for sports, and you get 796.357, classifying books on baseball. If you are interested in how to play baseball, or great games, great (and not so great) teams, or biographies of players, you will find most of the information under that number. As in all of life, there will be some exceptions. Some biographies may be in a biography section rather than among the baseball books. Older books may have just the basic 796 cataloging. However most books will follow the guidelines.

Under the number will be a line with one or more letters and sometimes some more numbers; 796.357 Sch57L. After you have found the number for the book that you want in the card catalog, you go to the shelves to look for that specific book. You may find a lot of books on the shelf with the number 796.357. You will find the books are arranged alphabetically by the letters and numbers underneath the call number. There are, of course, a number of specific rules about how these books are supposed to be arranged on the shelves, but those details are really only of concern to the librarians who put the books on the shelf. You really want just enough information to find your particular book. A general outline of the Dewey system follows.

THE DEWEY DECIMAL SYSTEM:

001–099: Information Retrieval. You will find encyclopedias, most almanacs, bibliographies, and books on computers (which are information retrieval systems) here. Also here are materials on journalism, writing, and a few other subjects. Oddly, the books on UFOs, the Loch Ness monster and other phenomena are here, as well.

100–199: *Philosophy and Psychology.* Besides books on philosophy and psychology, this section includes pop-psychology books, i.e., how to be assertive, happy, not timid, loving, not too loving (co-dependent), and so on. There are also materials in this area on parapsychology, the occult, and witchcraft.

200–299: *Religion.* Materials on all the religions of the world, past and present, are grouped here. You will find information on Christianity and all the various groupings of Christians (Catholics, Mormons, Protestants, Quakers, and many others), and on all the sects of the Moslem religion. You can learn about Judaism, Sikhism, Hinduism, Buddhism and others. Books on religions that are no longer observed are here, which means that material on Greek, Roman, Nordic and other mythology is classified under this number.

300–399: *Social Sciences.* This area covers everything from families (nuclear, step, adopted, divorced, and every other version you can think of), to economics (history of labor movements, family finances, the stock market, real estate), to government (how it does or doesn't work, political movements, the law, the armed forces, police, FBI, etc.), to crime. Education, including test books for the GED, SAT, ACT, and so on are included. The final subdivisions in this section are for marriages and weddings, and folktales. Of course, there are a few odds and ends in between.

400–499: *Language.* Here are the assorted dictionaries, thesauri, books on grammar and punctuation, and all of the books needed to learn various foreign languages.

500–599: *Pure Sciences.* Mathematics, physics, astronomy, meteorology, paleontology, botany, and biology, and so on are covered here. Books on wild animals are in this number range as well.

600–699: Applied Sciences. Medicine and engineering, as well as other applied sciences such as cooking, gardening, raising and training domestic animals such as dogs, cats, and cockatiels are found here. Also, materials on agriculture and animal husbandry, electronics (there will be some more computer books here), carpentry, upholstery, child rearing, and car repair may be found. The gardening books in the 600's tell how to compost, keep pests and weeds out, cultivate vegetables or fruits, and grow flowers. Those neat books with pictures of classic cars, rockets, and powerful planes are in this area, as are books on CB and ham radios, television, and how to fix your VCR. Other books in this area tell you how to restore an old house or build a new one, or how to build an addition to your current house. You can read about solar energy, wind power, wood stoves, welding, and masonry. The 600's are full of all kinds of odd and interesting things.

700–799: The Arts. Art history and information on famous artists and their works are in the 700's. How-to books are here, i.e., photography, stained glass work, jewelry making and folk arts such as tole painting. Arts and crafts books are here also: quilting, weaving, woodcarving, origami, doll and dollhouse making, embroidery, and more. There are some knitting, crocheting, and sewing books here as well. If you can't find what you are looking for, other such materials are located in the 600's as applied sciences. There are gardening books in the 700's, mostly with a slant toward landscaping and garden layout, with an emphasis on flowers and shrubs. This is also the area with flower arranging, and dried and pressed flower art. Theater arts and music books are here. You will find books on Mozart, Elvis, The Beatles, and your favorite movie stars or movie monsters. There are books on folk songs, acting, and how to put on clown makeup. You will also find sports and sports stars in the 700's.

800–899: Literature. Poetry, plays, and great literature through the ages, books on how to write (novels, short stories, poetry, mysteries, romances, suspense, your autobiography, for children, for adults, etc.), humor and satire books are in the 800's, as are books on public speaking and other miscellany.

900–999: History and Geography. Historical, cultural information and travel information is available here for all the states in the United States and for all the countries in the world. Travel books are located in the first part of the 900's. These not only include books on what to do and see in Paris and China, but also books on cruises, vacationing, shipwrecks, pirates and exploring. The entire history of the world, from ancient to modern times, through war and peace, depression and prosperity can be found in the 900's. The 920's also have biographical information, i.e., collective biographies on like groups of people; presidents, scientists, saints, and so on. Also here are books on the family from the point of view of genealogy, heraldry, and family names. Books on Native American tribes are here plus books on each state and all countries.

Biographies. Technically, according to the Library of Congress, biographies belong in the 900's, or, more recently, in the subject area in which the person became famous. In reality, most public libraries choose to keep them separate. They usually are placed after the end of the 900's and are arranged alphabetically by the subject's name.

There you have it—a brief (or maybe not so brief) run-down of the Dewey Decimal System. Keep this in mind: some subjects cross over to different areas of the collection. For example, books on drug addiction or alcoholism might be found in the 100's (psychology), the 300's (impact on society or society's impact on addiction) and in the 600's (medical aspects of addiction). Also, the Dewey Decimal System has gone through over twenty editions. The world has changed a lot since Melvil Dewey (1851–1931) first developed the system, and subjects have been reclassified, sometimes shifting to another area from one edition to the next of the same book. Computer books moved from applied science (the 621's), to information systems (the 001's). Now they have begun to migrate back into the 621's. As you research various subjects, or just browse, you will find other oddities that make the system less than fully unified. Familiarity with the Dewey Decimal Classification System alone cannot guarantee you access to necessary research materials. You also must understand the card catalog or computerized catalog.

It is important to be aware that Dewey is not a monolithic and uniform system. Individual libraries may make classification decisions specific to that library. One may decide to have a separate biography section; another may not. One library may decide to keep their adult and juvenile non-fiction separate while another may decide to combine the two. There are no public or school libraries exactly alike. Each one will be unique.

THE LIBRARY OF CONGRESS SYSTEM

The Library of Congress System is also based upon subject classification, but Library of Congress (LC) "numbers" start with letters, go to numbers, and often end with the copyright date. So, an LC number might look like this: HQ1170.G66 1994. It is the first letter that defines the primary classification. The number that follows further modifies the subject. Unlike Dewey libraries, Library of Congress libraries seldom pull things into separate areas. Fiction and biographies are shelved according to their assigned numbers, whereas in most Dewey libraries fiction and biographies are shelved separately.

A: *General Works.* This area includes encyclopedias (AE), dictionaries (AG), indexes (AI), and newspapers (AN), among others.

B: *Philosophy, Psychology and Religion.*

C: *Auxiliary Sciences of History.* This includes things like the history of civilization (CB), heraldry (CR), genealogy (CS), and biography (CT), as well as other subjects.

D: *History: General and Old World.* This is generally divided by country and region.

E–F: *History of the Western Hemisphere.*

G: *Geography, Anthropology and Recreation.* It is here you will find maps and   atlases, human ecology, manners and customs, and sports and games.

H: *Social Sciences.* Books and materials on finance (HG), families and marriage (HQ), communities (HT), and other social science topics are here.

J: *Political Science.*

K: *Law.*

L: *Education.* Here you will find materials on the history of education (LA), the theory and practice of education (LB), and institutions of education.

M: *Music.*

N: *Fine Arts.* Sculpture (NB), drawing (NC) and painting (ND), and decorative arts (NK) are in this section.

P: *Language and Literature.*

Q: *Science.* All of the hard sciences are here: math (QA), astronomy (QB), physics (QC), chemistry (QD), microbiology (QR), and so on.

S: *Agriculture.*
T: *Technology.* This area includes such subjects as engineering, construction, aeronautics, and home economics.
U: *Military Science.*
V: *Naval Science.*
Z: *Bibliography and Library Science.*

This general outline of how the two major classification systems in this country are structured will help you locate an area or a subject, but the Good Detective will need much more to conduct serious research. Therefore, we will push on to the card catalog and its equivalents to see how these cataloging systems *really* enable you to do good detective work.

Chapter Three

Read Any Good Catalog Cards Lately?
The Card Catalog And Its Equivalents

Okay, you know a little about the Dewey Decimal System and the Library of Congress System. You spend a fair amount of time in your local library, and readily stroll over to your favorite sections without needing to look up the numbers. If you want to learn a martial art you go to 796.81. If you still have some hope of training your dog, you go to 636.7. If you are bound and determined to make yourself a quilt (or talk your mother into making it) to take with you to college in two years, you go to the 746.46 shelf. If you always wanted a dinosaur for a pet you go to 567—better yet, go to the adult fiction shelves (alphabetical by author) and read *Jurassic Park* by Michael Crichton. That should cure you of that notion.

When you have to do research for a paper, however, a quick rundown of the Dewey Decimal System just will not be enough. Knowing religion is in the 200's or science in the 500's cuts too wide a swath. If you really want to compare the dietary laws of Judaism, the Mormon Church, and Islam, you need to pinpoint your topic. Similarly, browsing through the 500's could take a lifetime if you are looking for the Engineering Rule of Rounding. The spines of several thousand books would dance before your eyes before one leapt out with the information you require. The card catalog solves this dilemma. It works with the Dewey Decimal System and the Library of Congress System to provide the location of a given book or topic.

The card catalog allows you to look books up by author, title, or subject. Some libraries arrange their card catalogs as a single alphabetical unit, with author, title and subject cards interfiled. Many libraries maintain separate catalogs or sections for authors, titles, and subjects. There can be other combinations. Each book has several cards. At the very least, a book will have an author card (if there is a specific author) and a title card, so you can learn where the book is shelved if you know either its name or the writer's name. Non-fiction books also have one or more subject cards. Once you locate the author, or title, or subject card for the book you want, the card indicates what Dewey or Library of Congress number is assigned to it. You know exactly what shelf in the library holds your book.

Many people know how to read a basic catalog card. Or do they? The Good Detective needs to know that there is more to a catalog card than just a title and Dewey or LC number. When you look up books for a research project, you should net the maximum reward for your time and trouble. When looking something up quickly, you just check the Dewey numbers for two or three titles. Then browse the shelves in your subject area to see what you can see. But when you are on a treasure hunt, and especially at the start of the trail, look very closely at your first few hits. Note the Dewey numbers not only to locate specific books, but also to observe a pattern of locations.

Remember, the Dewey Decimal and Library of Congress Systems are *subject* classification systems. You approach your search expecting books on the same general subject to be close together on the shelves. Can you assume all the books on a subject have the same subject cards? Sounds reasonable, but no, you cannot. Most libraries fill out only a few catalog cards per book. Thick wads of cards per book take up too much space and are expensive. It also takes a lot of work to get them filed. In most libraries, a non-fiction book

Ask for what you really want

has as few as one or two subject cards, or as many as three or four. For example, you may have looked up flower gardening, and found the title *Edible Flowers from Garden to Palate* by Barash. The subject headings assigned to this book are 1. *Cookery (flowers)*, 2. *Flower gardening*, and 3. *Herb gardening*. If *cookery (flowers)* is closer to what you are interested in than *flower gardening*, you switch over and try that subject heading.

The Dewey or catalog card number thus serves not only

ANATOMY OF A CATALOG CARD

These are examples of catalog cards. Some cards may have more or less information and some may look a little different. You can use catalog cards to find a particular book. You can also use them as springboards to other books if you follow the clues they contain.

This is an author main entry card. Some books don't have a specific author. Then the title will be first and it will be considered the main entry. If this is the card you are looking at in a catalog then you looked it up by the author. Check to see what other books the author has written.

> 641.6
> B
>
> Barash, Cathy Wilkinson, 1949-
>   Edible flowers : from garden to palate /
> Cathy Wilkinson Barash. -- Golden, Colo. :
> Fulcrum Pub., c1993.
>   xiii, 250 p. : col. ill. ; 24 cm.
>
>   1. Cookery (Flowers) 2. Flower gardening.
>   3. Herb gardening. I. Title.

>   Cookery (Flowers)
>
> 641.6
> B
>
> Barash, Cathy Wilkinson, 1949-
>   Edible flowers : from garden to palate /
> Cathy Wilkinson Barash. -- Golden, Colo. :
> Fulcrum Pub., c1993.
>   xiii, 250 p. : col. ill. ; 24 cm.
>
>   1. Cookery (Flowers) 2. Flower gardening.
>   3. Herb gardening. I. Title.

This is a subject card. It is the basic (main entry) card with a subject heading typed at the top of the card and the card is filed by this subject heading.

At the bottom of the card there is a list of all the entries beyond the main entry where you will be able to find this book listed. For this book there will be three subject cards and a title card. That is 5 cards total and 5 possible ways to look up this book. Check the other subject headings to see if there are other books on your topic.

This is a title card so this will be filed by the title in the catalog.

Notice the classification number. Sometimes it will be worth your while to browse in that area. It is almost like finding another subject heading.

>   Edible flowers
>
> 641.6
> B
>
> Barash, Cathy Wilkinson, 1949-
>   Edible flowers : from garden to palate /
> Cathy Wildinson Barash. -- Golden, Colo. :
> Fulcrum Pub., c1993.
>   xiii, 250 p. : col. ill. ; 24 cm.
>
>   1. Cookery (Flowers) 2. Flower gardening.
>   3. Herb gardening. I. Title.

as a locator for a specific subject or book, but as a spring-board to other places to investigate. The list of subject head-ings serves to lead you to related, perhaps more pertinent, subjects. Of course, this applies to non-fiction, as fiction usu-ally has only an author and title card for each book. If you want a good novel about the Revolutionary War, the card catalog may not be the answer.

It may be possible in your library to look at another card catalog system called a shelflist, though in most libraries this cataloging tool is not available to the public. When it is, it can be a very handy reference tool. A shelflist is a com-pletely separate card catalog from the author/title/subject catalog. The shelflist has only one card for each book, filed by the catalog (Dewey or LC) number, in exactly the order the books are shelved in the library.

While on any given day a book may be checked out, these cards are always in place, and thus offer a full picture of the books in a given location. If you browse the shelves in an area, some books are checked out, some left on tables, others are in carts to go back on the shelves, and a few fugitives are hidden wherever books migrate to when they are not in their proper place. The shelflist gives you a full picture of what exists in that library, even those items not immediately available. You identify a particular book or books, reserve or request the titles, and get them as soon as they are re-turned or located.

There are a couple of "ifs" involved in the use of a shelflist. It's only useful *if* it is open to the public and *if* you have time to wait for a book to be returned. Skip the shelflist if the report you are writing is due the day after tomorrow. Use the shelflist only if you know enough about the library cataloging system to look at that area. All in all, the shelflist can be useful if it's there, but few people will miss it if it's not. This type of search does come up again when we talk about computerized catalogs.

The major springboards to use when you look at a cata-log card are the subject headings. You make your first "hit" in the catalog—a friend gave you a title, or you happen on a real subject heading, or you stumble over a book on the floor that seems a good possibility and you decide to see if the author wrote any other relevant books. Stop. Take a moment to look at the other subject headings on the card for this book. Just as with the edible flowers book, these subject headings may lead you to related headings that bear on your topic. Do this for every book you look up. You may uncover more pertinent subject headings.

Some subject headings change over the years. Like dresses and color schemes and sports, words go in and out of fashion. One year a particular term might be in vogue. Five years, or even as little as two years later, a completely different word may be chosen for a book covering the same information. *The Nontoxic Home* was published in 1986. It is cataloged with the number 615.9 (a health number) and carries the subject headings *toxicology—popular works, product safety, consumer education,* and *poisoning–prevention. The Healthy Home,* published just three years later, in 1989, is cataloged in 643.7 and has subject headings of *indoor air pollution—health aspects,* and *housing and health.* Both books discuss the health aspects of materials we use in our homes, and both give "recipes" for alternative, natural and nontoxic cleaning supplies and other items. Both of these books are helpful if you have to do a report on environmental illness, or if you suspect that you have an environmental illness or allergy, but they are located in totally different places in the library under completely different subject headings.

Sometimes a search can be like a chess game—these two books are about two moves away from each other if you follow the subject heading leads. And the paths will lead to other pertinent books that share these subject headings.

At this point, at risk of life and limb (they are, after all, my colleagues), I will say a word about catalogers, the people who assign the numbers and subject headings. They are not like the librarians you meet at the front desk. Now don't get me wrong. They are very nice people, but the fact remains that nobody can please everybody all the time. There will be times when we don't agree with a decision the cataloger makes. Nevertheless, the Good Detective has to operate within the framework the catalogers construct. It can be like a game of Dungeons & Dragons™. The catalogers are the Dungeon Masters. You must explore every nook and cranny to find the treasure, plumbing the maze as they have constructed it.

There are automated catalogs that function as card catalogs. Some libraries use microfiche. They film all the card information and update it periodically. You read it through a machine, but it takes up a lot less space than a regular card catalog. Functionally, searching this way is very similar to searching a regular card catalog.

Very different is the true on-line, or computerized catalog. A variety of computer catalogs exist. Some call for you to type in your request on a keyboard. Others have you touch the screen display to indicate your selection. There are a number of systems more or less similar to each other. After you master the intricacies of the systems at whatever library or libraries you are using (school, public, college or university) you may decide they all boil down to familiar ground. You adapt your searches to the computer system, but you still search author, title and subject. If you look further, you will find computerized catalogs may have the ability to search by catalog number (like the shelflist). Most computerized catalogs also indicate if a book is checked out.

The most exciting and helpful capability that computerized catalogs offer is the possibility of keyword searching. If the computer catalog that you are working with allows *keyword* or *boolean* searching, you can search for a book by a significant word or phrase, even if that word or phrase is not the first word, or even part of the title. The computer scans the author, title, and subject fields, and also any summary statements or publication information that is part of the description of the book or item. For example, one day I thought of a book I wanted to look at, but I couldn't remember the title. I did remember that it had something to do with ponies going oink. When I did a keyword search using the words "ponies" and "oink" the computer came up with the title *Real Ponies Don't Go Oink* by Patrick McManus, call number 817M. That was it! I got my book. If I had tried to find that in a card catalog, I wouldn't have had a chance. I would have needed to know the first word, "Real" or the author. A title search done in a computerized catalog would also have needed the first word.

Keyword searching helped another library searcher, in this case a mystery lover who happened on an exciting book that was one of a series, *The Brown Bagger Mysteries*. Each volume is by a different author, and other titles in the series were not listed in the book he had read. A keyword search on *brown bagger* brought up only one title. Apparently none of the other computer catalog listings for the different books included the series name. The mystery lover performed another keyword search on the publisher's name, *Council Oak*. This brought up 16 entries, five of which turned out to be part of *The Brown Bagger Mysteries*. Of course, this would not have worked as well if the publisher had hundreds of titles out.

A keyword search also comes in handy if you are not certain of the actual subject heading for what you want. Only certain words serve as subject headings. This is called *controlled vocabulary*. It's like getting onto an interstate highway. You can't get on from just any street, but must enter from a street with an entrance ramp. Only certain words are the entrance ramps for a subject search. A lot of other words come immediately and logically to mind, and seem most reasonable on the surface. But they won't work if they are not actual, authorized subject headings. A keyword search can function as your treasure map, to uncover the correct entry ramp or subject term. One man wanted books on etymology, the branch of linguistics that deals with the origins of words. This seems straightforward enough—except that a subject search for *etymology* brought up nothing. How could this be? He went on to a keyword search on *etymology*, which brought up a number of titles. Looking at the subject headings he found that the real subject search should have been for *English language—etymology*.

Often a keyword search will bring up more titles than you can deal with if the significant word is not unique or specific. If the computer tells you that the word you searched pulled up 1,382 titles, you know you need another word to narrow the search. A person doing a report on fidelity in marriage didn't want books on divorce or infidelity, but only on fidelity. A keyword search brought up 31 titles, three of which had to do with her actual subject. The other 29 titles had to do with high fidelity recordings and equipment. So there are times you must modify your search with at least one other term, or a date, or something else to limit what you bring up. Then, as in the search for *etymology* you can swing over to the subject search you actually want.

Yet another use for keyword searching, depending on your library's software, is to specify a format. In my particular library at this moment (the numbers change almost daily), if I look up *compact disks* I will pull up a list of 4,174 entries. More than I care to browse through. A keyword search could narrow the list by composer, or performer, or perhaps by language or type of music. It may allow me to look up individual song titles as well. Keyword searches also may allow you to find audio tapes and video cassettes.

Not all computer systems have the same keyword search capabilities. It is well worth the Good Detective's time to become fully acquainted with your library's computer catalog or card catalog. They are tools. Learn to use them and make them work for you. Take advantage of the classes libraries offer on the use of their computerized system. If there are no classes, go to the information desk and ask the librarian to teach you how to use the system. As you become familiar with it you can ask for more,

"Will it do this?" or "Can I look something up by that?" The more you understand the rules the computer follows the better you will be able to manipulate it.

Chapter Four

Springboards!
Basic Reference Sources

ENCYCLOPEDIAS

Where do you go when you first get an assignment? Many students start with an encyclopedia—and stop with an encyclopedia. After all, the articles are short (very important), contain a lot of information (also important), and if you take good notes you can do your whole report or worksheet or questionnaire from that one encyclopedia article. Right? Wrong!

You may find everything you want in an encyclopedia. However, most teachers are well aware of the basic information in articles in *The World Book Encyclopedia, The Americana,* and other general encyclopedias. If your sights are set on earning better than a C for your effort, you must look farther. Sometimes teachers give assignments that specifically forbid use of an encyclopedia as a source. Or they might require that you use a certain number of sources (the teacher perhaps hoping that you will run out of encyclopedias and have to look farther).

Does this mean that you should not use encyclopedias? No way! It only means you should look at other sources as well. Encyclopedias are very important. They can be useful even if your teacher requires five sources on your bibliography, none of them encyclopedias. It is not that you can't use an encyclopedia, it means that you use it for background information, or as a springboard. Use it to find the other places you can go to to track down information. It can lead you to the best trail to do your research knowledgeably and effectively.

Use encyclopedias the same way you use the card or computer catalog. Wring from them every last piece of information. There are many good general encyclopedias on the market. Your library may have just one set or it may have four or five. If your library has different sets, take the time to look at all of them. This works best if you haven't put off doing the assignment until the night before it is due. Each encyclopedia will present good, concise, readable, information-packed articles, but with different emphases.

It is a mistake to think that if you see one article in an encyclopedia you have seen them all. Articles in different encyclopedias are written by different scholars, each with a slightly different focus. One gives more complete dates, or better pictures (important in some instances). Another does a little better with coverage of countries or people. A third may be better at listing names or places for further research (springboards!).

If you are assigned a report on a Black American author, and your mind has gone totally blank, check the *World Book* under *Black Americans*. At the end of the article there will be lists of people; scientists, politicians, athletes, entertainers, writers, and others. Need to find a British commander in the Revolutionary War in America? How about women suffrage leaders? The articles on these subjects and others list people and related subject articles at the end. These are not all encompassing listings, but they can be a great help. Other encyclopedias will have different strengths. Which one is most helpful will differ from one assignment to another.

Each set of encyclopedias has an index volume, which people sometimes ignore. After all, the whole set is alphabetical. If you want to look up China, you just go to the C encyclopedia. Once you've read the article you know everything there is to know about China. Right? Well, it's a good start, but if you go to the index volume you will find a number of "see also" references. These may refer you to *Architecture (Chinese)*, *T'ang Dynasty*, and *Family (Traditional Families in Other Cultures)*. Now, in addition to the C volume, we could find more in the A, T, and F volumes. And there are many other references, ranging from agriculture to drama to religion to ancient trade routes, plus a lot in between. One of these other references may be closer to what you want than the original article.

Cross-references in the index volume can tell you when you are looking up the wrong thing. For instance, your whole family may have always said *Chiropody* but if you don't find that in the C encyclopedia, check the index volume. There you will learn that you must look in the P volume under *Podiatry*. And of course, all of your friends have always talked of *Chiromancy* but the index volume lets you know you must look under *Palmistry* to find it in the encyclopedia.

The index volume can help you find or verify spellings. Yes, dictionaries do that, but not all dictionaries will include names such as *Kruschev* (or is it *Khruschev*?). Oops! According to the index it's *Khrushchev*.

The index also gives the correct form to find an unusual name. Question: do you find *Leonardo da Vinci* under *Vinci*, *Da Vinci*, or *Leonardo*? Answer: different encyclopedias may choose different forms. In many cases the articles in the encyclopedia conclude with "see" references, but other references may only be in the index. As you can *see*, the "see" and "see also" references in the index can be most important for the student. The index to the *Encyclopaedia Britannica*, for example, is incredibly comprehensive. It has place names that are not even in atlases or gazetteers. What's a gazetteer? See the section in this book on gazetteers and geographic dictionaries. The *Britannica Micropaedia* and index contain odd and arcane bits of information that could be difficult to locate elsewhere even for those with a background in the topic.

One librarian could find nothing on *Sturm und Drang* even though she already knew that it was a German literary movement. In that particular library none of the books on Germany or literature included the term. It was not until she turned to the *Encyclopaedia Britannica* that she was able to find a definition.

The index of an encyclopedia can be very helpful, even to the person in a hurry, who may consider it a time-consuming extra step. Searching an index only takes a few minutes. It offers invaluable information and tips on possible directions to go with your paper or research, and lays out the path to pursue those directions.

In addition to the many encyclopedias in hard copy, that is, the printed page, there are also encyclopedias on CD-ROM. These can be really neat and helpful. You do a keyword search and the screen instantly displays the article. CD-ROM encyclopedias largely have multimedia capabilities, i.e., the pictures incorporate sound and motion.

Whatever encyclopedias are available to you, use them fully. Whether you are doing your homework or trying to find out what color to paint your duck decoy, get everything you can out of your encyclopedia. Read the article. Scan the "see" and "see also" references. Check the index. The Good Detective will come away not only with the information but also with clues to other sources.

Specialized Encyclopedias

Besides the ever-so-popular general encyclopedias, there are a huge number of specialized encyclopedias. Some libraries don't have any of these, some only have one or two. College and university libraries usually have many. Each specialized encyclopedia covers a given topic, ranging from animals to politics to religion to science. The articles are in much greater detail than in general encyclopedias, but the form is the same: alphabetical by topic. We will discuss just a few specialized encyclopedias, to give you a taste of the variety that is available.

Do you have to write a paper on a particular artist or art movement? *The Encyclopedia of World Art* should have just the information you need. Like a "regular" encyclopedia it is a huge multivolume set, but it specializes in just one subject area—art. Do you need to know about electromagnetism or aerothermodynamics? *The McGraw Hill Encyclopedia of Science and Technology* may answer your questions. Do you need a floor plan of King Herod's Temple to teach your Sunday school class? Try *The Encyclopedia Judaica.* Do you want to know what happened at Nauvoo, Illinois to make it important to more than 8.5 million people around the world? Check *The Encyclopedia of Mormonism.* Did you always want a slender loris for a pet and need to know what it eats? Look it up in *Grzimek's Animal Life Encyclopedia.*

There are encyclopedias for the social sciences, endangered species, humankind, mathematics, politics, geology, computer science and technology, engineering, mythology, monsters, reptiles, earthquakes and volcanoes, and many more. If your library has any of these they can be incredibly informative. They are also expensive and occupy a lot of shelf space, so not all libraries have all of them, but if you didn't know they exist you wouldn't look for them and a Good Detective never wants to miss a source as good as these.

DICTIONARIES

Most people use dictionaries to find the meaning of a word or to verify its spelling. In fact, the dictionary is a veritable compendium (look it up!) of all kinds of information. As with encyclopedias, different dictionaries give you different types of information. What might you find in a dictionary?

1. Correct spellings and accepted variant spellings.

2. Definitions of words and phrases.

3. How to pronounce the word.

4. Pictures. Some dictionaries include pictures of the item, as well as charts of weights and measures, metric conversion, etc.

5. Etymology. Derivations of words, like *beef* from the French *buef*, or *cow* from the German *kuo*, and sometimes the year or epoch in which the word came into usage.

6. Foreign words and phrases commonly in use. This could come in handy when you want to impress your friends, *n'est-ce pas*?

7. Biographical entries. These are usually very short for quick reference.

8. Geographical entries. These will also be very short.

9. Information on punctuation and grammar.

10. Signs and symbols in various subject areas, for example, astronomy, mathematics, physics and so on.

11. Forms of address—in case you get to meet the Pope (Your Holiness), or the president (Mr. President).

12. Abbreviations. Did you think *CD* just referred to *compact disk*? It could also mean *certificate of deposit* and other things as well. *ERA* could mean *Equal Rights Amendment* or *earned run average*.

13. A history of the English language.

14. A history of the Indo-European languages and people.

15. Listings of colleges and universities and their addresses.

16. Listings of foreign alphabets.

In general, of course, dictionaries are best for spellings and definitions and information on the etymology of a word, and can be helpful for grammar and punctuation. The rest is icing on the cake. No dictionary has all of the extras mentioned above, but most dictionaries will be very informative.

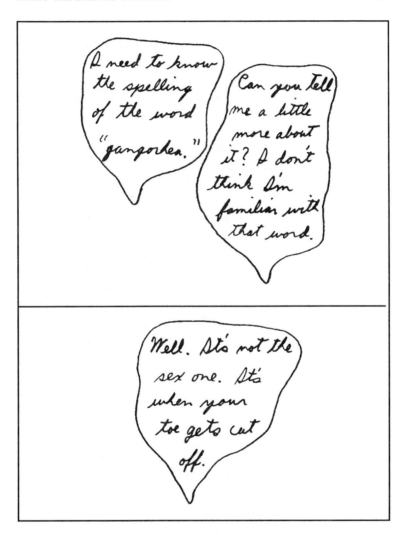

Specialized Dictionaries

Just as there are specialized encyclopedias, there are specialized dictionaries that include terms or information relevant to a particular field. Many of these words or phrases are unlikely to appear in a regular dictionary. There are medical dictionaries that cover diseases and medicines. The legal profession has a whole vocabulary of specialized terms which require the use of a legal dictionary. There are also science dictionaries, economics dictionaries, and many other subject-specific dictionaries.

There are picture dictionaries, and not just for children. The adult versions have highly detailed illustrations, such as cross sections of equipment or architecture. Each detail is labeled with its correct name. This can be especially helpful for people such as immigrants who live in a culture which speaks a different language than their native tongue, and also for people who want to refer to an object other than as a *thingamajig* or a *whatsit*. You can look at pictures of machinery and find the terms for different parts, or look up houses and buildings and find the correct architectural terms. Many of these words might show up in a regular dictionary, but without the picture. Imagine, for instance, a piece of wall that hangs down from the ceiling and doesn't go all the way to the floor. What do you call that, and how could you look it up in a regular dictionary? If *soffit* doesn't spring immediately to mind, a picture dictionary will help you.

There are dictionaries for acronyms, initials and abbreviations. You can look up abbreviations and initials in a regular dictionary and learn the most common two or three meanings. A specialized dictionary, however, has *all* the possible meanings for a given abbreviation or set of initials, no matter how uncommon. For example, remember the *CD* you looked up before? The regular dictionary talked about *Compact Disks* and *Certificates of Deposit*. In a dictionary of abbreviations you may find as many as 160 meanings. You learn that CD means *Convulsive Dose, Combination Drugs, Chief of Division, Cathedral, Canine Distemper* and a bunch of other things. If you always wanted to know what *AD* means when placed after a date you could look up those initials in a specialized dictionary and find that they mean *Anno Domini* (Latin for *In the year of Our Lord*), but you would have to sort this meaning out from well over a hundred other ADs including *Architectural Digest* (a magazine), *Art Direc-*

tor, Area Director, Automatic Display, Atomic Drive, and so on.

There are specialized dictionaries for slang, clichés and phrases. They give definitions, and also etymology, the study of when, where, and how words and phrases came to be.

There are dictionaries for synonyms, antonyms, homonyms, homophones (*rein, reign, rain*), palindromes (look it up, it's neat), rhyming dictionaries, crossword puzzle dictionaries, and thesauri. And of course, there are foreign language dictionaries: English-German, Spanish-English, English-Hebrew, and so on.

ALMANACS

Almanacs are interesting books. They cover as wide range of topics as many encyclopedias, but the information is presented in brief. What can you find there? Odd and esoteric morsels.

A general almanac will tell you what wins over what in a poker hand and your chances of drawing each hand. For the non-players among us (that includes me) the winning hands in ascending order are: one pair, two pair, three of a kind, straight, flush, full house, four of a kind, straight flush, royal flush. If I could just remember what a flush is. I guess I'll have to go look it up.

Do you want to know what day of the week you were born? Almanacs have perpetual calendars. They are, in general, especially good with lists and tables. An almanac may have a chronological table of landmark dates in world and United States history. You can find lists of major mountains, rivers, lakes, deserts, volcanoes, disasters. Also listed are winners of prizes and awards, including Nobel prize winners back to 1899, Pulitzer Prize winners, Miss America winners, Academy Award and Grammy Award winners, Olympic sports winners, Westminster Kennel Club winners, and Kentucky Derby winners. Almanacs have lists of people who excelled in various areas, lists of addresses (colleges, religious headquarters, political leaders), lists of inventions. Almanacs list statistical information: birth and death rates, how people died, marriage and divorce statistics, years of education for different segments of the population, and crime rates and prison population statistics. All sorts of information from the astronomical (what time will/did the sun rise on April 27th), to the zoological (If I visit my Aunt Gretchen in Toledo, Ohio this summer is there a zoo in that city and what are its major claims to fame?) is available in almanacs.

The information provided is very concise. Almanacs offer quick information bites. You can look up a president and find out when he was born, when he died, when he served and what his major accomplishments or political stands were, all in about one paragraph. In some cases this might be exactly what you are looking for. In other cases this might be the springboard you need to go further with your research.

Your library may also have (guess what!) specialized almanacs. Best known is *The Farmer's Almanac,* with weather and astronomy tied to planting and harvesting, recipes, and all sorts of down-home remedies and folklore. Other specialized almanacs include weather, business, energy, ethnic groups (Hispanic-American, African-American, Native American, etc.), sports almanacs, historical almanacs, and many others. Some of these have rather comprehensive information and some just quick information hits. Use of almanacs can provide a quick answer or a springboard to other sources or related subjects.

ATLASES

Where in the world is *that*?

Sometimes the question is "where in the world *was* that?" Either way, libraries have geographical sources that will help you plan a trip, gather information for reports, or find out

where, in relation to the rest of the world, your ancestors came from.

For trip planning there are things like *The Standard Highway Mileage Guide* (How many miles from here to Albuquerque?) or a good road atlas (What's the best, or fastest, or most scenic route to Atlanta?) A road atlas often includes mileage and driving times between major destinations.

Atlases and other geographical sources can help you with information for reports. What are the major products and mineral resources of southern Africa? What are the major products of the Australian subcontinent? What were the political boundaries in Europe before World War II?

Different kinds of atlases tell you different things. A commercial atlas such as *The Rand McNally Commercial Atlas*, besides maps and distance and driving times, offers information of interest to business people. This includes such data, often by city or county, as the number of households, income, and car registrations, sales by dollar amount and type (general merchandise, apparel, food, drugs, etc.), general income information, bank deposits, information on area businesses including numbers of employees, largest banks, largest insurance companies, largest industrial companies, and so on. One of the many functions this specialized almanac could provide is to help a person decide if they wanted to start a business in an area.

The World Atlas of Archaeology takes a geographer's view of archaeology. It uses pictures, drawings, maps, and text to discuss archaeological discoveries all over the world, including facts about people who once lived in these sites. *The Atlas of the Second World War* chronicles the war in pictures, maps and text. *The World Atlas of Architecture* shows both ancient and modern types of architecture throughout the world (houses and gardens, temples, churches, and public buildings) and discusses how styles were and are affected by the people, climate, resources, etc., of an area and how the architecture reflects the culture. *We The People: An Atlas of America's Ethnic Diversity* maps out the ethnic groups

which constitute the United States population, and discusses patterns of settlement and migration and general historical developments.

These are just a few of the variety of atlases available. Atlases can cover almost any subject, and can be very helpful to the Good Detective. Pictures and maps help bring a subject to life.

World atlases are excellent sources of information. The maps and indexes include more than just political information (cities, counties, states, nations, etc.). They also cover mountains, deserts, valleys, rivers and other geographical highlights. World atlases are often almost encyclopedic in the amount of information they contain.

As with encyclopedias, different atlases contain different information, so look in more than one if your library offers a variety. A world atlas may have an overview of the geologic history and makeup of the world including information on plate tectonics. It may have astronomical information to illustrate where the earth fits into the universe, in which case you will find star maps, information on the universe, the moon, the solar system and so on. A world atlas might have information on the biosphere and world climates, temperature ranges, vegetation, and meteorological data. World population and population density, language groupings and ethnic groupings, world food crop ranges, famine and child mortality rates can be found, along with world resources and industrial distribution.

Be sure to check the copyright date when you use a current atlas, as opposed to a historical atlas. Just a few years can make a big difference in the information. Some of the countries shown in a 1988 atlas will be quite different from the countries and political boundaries in a 1994 atlas.

That brings us to historical atlases, which have maps and information about specific time periods and specific locations. You can find historical atlases for biblical times, the American Revolution, and other times and places. We tend to think of atlases as collections of maps, but they also describe political events, how people lived, and the effect of historic events on people's lives. They may contain statistical information. Some maps show how borders and shapes of countries changed over a period of time.

During the 40 years between 1910 and 1950, the borders and countries of Europe changed shape many times. They continue to change today. These are not just dry changes of lines on a map; these changes and how they come about have a direct effect on the lives (and deaths) of the people inhabiting those areas. Boundary changes impel people to emigrate, with consequences also for the people in the countries which receive the immigrants.

And on, and on. Historical atlases have good information for school reports, provide excellent pleasure reading (for people who like non-fiction), and also can be very helpful for tracing family histories.

Historical atlases are interesting for another reason; geographers describe history differently than historians, who look primarily at politics and economics. A geographer's perspective considers how the world's physical makeup (land, climate, natural resources, etc.) influences people and the patterns of history. Atlases provide a visual explanation of both the physical characteristics of the world and the patterns of activity that take place.

This brings us to another point, one the Good Detective should always think about when doing research. We know geographers can give us a different perspective or slant on the world. Military historians take a different view of historic events than do political and economic historians. Who else might take a different view of history, both past and current? Looking at a subject from a variety of perspectives gives you a broader view. Sometimes an author's bias or personal opinions affects what he or she writes. The Good Detective must learn to recognize when an author is trying to give information versus when that same author is trying to shape the reader's opinion. There also will be times an author is not consciously trying to sway your opinion, yet his or her account reflects some personal bias. The Good Detective needs to be sensitive to opinion forming words (or opinionated words) as opposed to objective descriptions and accounts.

GAZETTEERS AND GEOGRAPHIC DICTIONARIES

A gazetteer, or geographic dictionary, alphabetically lists both natural and man-made places in the world. In a gazetteer you might find cities, towns, countries, counties, parishes, states, rivers, valleys, mountains, deserts, and numerous other places. It's a dictionary of places. These include historical places, which have since disappeared, and places with names that have changed over the years. The entries offer brief, pertinent information about the place, and locate it relative to other places. Gazetteers do not normally include maps. The entries in gazetteers and geographic dictionaries can be good springboards to get you started on a search.

These and other geographical sources are ideal for the Good Detective, since tracking clues and information is much like following a map. The sport of orienteering would be the perfect hobby for the Good Detective for just that reason. What is orienteering? Well, *The New Encyclopaedia Britannica* (15th ed. c1992) says it is an "outdoor competitive sport similar to cross country running, but with emphasis on map-reading and direction-finding skills." It goes on to say that it can also be done with bikes, canoes and on horseback. But to really excel as orienteers/detectives/fact trackers we need to use more than springboards. We need to learn to negotiate mazes, so let us go on to the next chapter.

Chapter Five

In Short, Mazes: Indexes, Pathfinders, And Bibliographies

A search through indexes, pathfinders and bibliographies creates mazes of the sort you find in fantasy role playing games. One hit moves you in one direction. Another hit takes you in a different direction. Maybe the next hit will take you further in the original direction. Each curve in the maze gives you more information.

You may prefer to think of it as an archeological dig. You pore through layers of information until the accumulation lets you derive the answers at the end. Whereupon you write your paper or do your project. Like all mazes, indexes, pathfinders and bibliographies do not always lead in a straight line, but they are the best sources we have right now for finding information.

MAGAZINE INDEXES

Indexes provide the handiest way to find a fact, figure or bit of information, so we will cover these first. We won't talk about encyclopedia indexes again, but remember keyword searches on computers? Using an index is akin to a manual (pre-computer age) keyword search. A computer scans all the words in a record or text to find the keyword it is searching for (sometimes programs skip common words like *the, a, or,* etc.). An index is composed of *selected* words; subjects, phrases, names, whatever, which an individual has selected from the text as significant or descriptive. For a successful hunt, you must hone in more specifically on what you want than is necessary for a computer keyword search.

You are probably familiar with a book index, found in the last few pages of a non-fiction book, and providing a quick route to information. The table of contents at the beginning can also be helpful, but chapter headings are more general categories. You have to read or scan the text for specifics. With an index you can go directly to the details you want by manually looking up the keyword.

There are indexes for magazine articles, newspaper articles, poems, quotations, and other things. Unlike a book index, these indexes are not generally housed in the same volumes or issues they are indexing.

Magazine indexes are quite commonly found in libraries and are among the most popular indexes. Why? While a book is usually published a year or two after its completion, magazine articles tend to be current, which could be very important for some research. Also, magazine indexes cover a number of magazines, and so draw from many sources. A book index covers only that book, and an encyclopedia index that particular encyclopedia set. So, a magazine index will be both broader and more up-to-date than a book index.

The Readers' Guide to Periodical Literature is the magazine index most often found in public and school libraries. It indexes about 250 magazines. There is an average lag time of some six weeks from the appearance of a magazine to the time the articles are referenced in the index in your local library. You find the articles you want by searching for a subject term. This is one of those times when you may have to take several guesses if you are not sure what term will be selected as the main subject. Once you do find the subject you want, you get a list of articles on that subject, and you may also get some "see also" references. Don't ignore these. Scan them for another subject heading of interest, or one

SAMPLE SEARCH PATH I

I'm interested in building or buying an electric car. Is there any current information that might help me with that?
s=subject search
k=keyword search

===

COMPUTERIZED CATALOG
s=Electric car
The computer said to search under s=Automobiles, Electric. 4 hits, 3 of which were pertinent. Another subject heading in one of the hits was s=Electric-Vehicles 8 hits, 7 of which were pertinent. There was also a referral to s=Solar Vehicles. No different hits. Didn't use keyword searching.

Yield=10 good hits on pertinent books.
4 books were immediately available, 2 could be pulled in from other locations within a day, and the rest could be reserved.

CD-ROM PERIODICAL INDEX
k=Electric Automobiles. 2 hits. Subject headings in the abstract prompted a subject search. s=Electric Power Automobiles. 17 hits.

Note: Why did the keyword search come up with 2 hits when the subject search on the same words come up with 17 hits? Because on this system the words "electric automobiles" were searched as a phrase rather than as individual words. A later search on "electric and automobiles" turned up 57 hits.

READERS' GUIDE TO PERIODICAL LITERATURE
s=Electric Vehicles referred searcher to s=Automobiles, Electric. 20 hits. This was a sample search on the 1993 volume only. Subsequent searches of 1994 and 1992 issues yielded 52 more hits.

Note: Even though the CD-ROM system covered 5 plus years and this was only one year of Readers' Guide it yielded proportionately more hits because it indexes more periodicals than the CD-ROM system available at this library. Other computerized indexing systems may yield more or fewer hits.

GOVERNMENT DOCUMENTS
k=Electric Automobile-1 hit, Electric Vehicles-129 hits. Most of these were not applicable. Electric Automobiles-56 hits. Some of interest.

ENCYCLOPEDIAS
These had very little on electric cars. No help.

RESULTS: Best sources for this subject were the periodicals and current books. Several relevant hits.

even closer to what you want. Suppose a science teacher invited you to be in a solar car race. Never mind that the other entries are paid for with university dollars and built by engineering students and faculty. You're going to figure out how to build your own. You are going to have to follow through on a lot of "see also" references.

Once you find the subject you want you will find certain information in the citations. This will include titles of articles, and where a title isn't very descriptive there may be an explanation of what the article is about. Usually these explanations are short, not more than four to six words. There will be some other information, such as the author's name, and whether or not the article is illustrated, and then the crucial information—what magazine the article is in, the date of that issue, and the page number. After you find your citations you close the index and go get the magazines that have the articles with the information you are seeking.

Unfortunately, most libraries can neither afford to buy nor do they have space to keep as many magazines as are indexed in *The Readers' Guide,* but it is still a good start. Some libraries solve the space problem by offering magazines on microfilm or microfiche. Even if your library doesn't have the magazine you need, copy the citation. You may be able to find the material at another library. While this book is aimed primarily at public and school library users, college, university and community college libraries will often let visitors use their facilities. This can be a great boon to the Good Detective and is rather like going into a candy store. There is so much to choose from!

Another type of magazine indexing is available on computer CD-ROM disks. Different companies sell CD-ROM indexing systems with various features. The major advantage of these computerized indexes is that the computer does the searching for you, using the keyword search capability. It is not just a search on article titles, which often are not very descriptive. The searches also scan another major feature of a CD-ROM system, the abstract.

Many systems don't just index articles, but also summarize, or abstract them. This offers two major advantages. After you read the abstract, you have a clearer idea of subject matter without having to find the magazine and read a complete article. Your subsequent computer keyword search can employ a more descriptive citation than just the title and bibliographic information.

Your next move will be influenced by the system your library has purchased and how much they spent on it. You might leave the computer with your list of citations and go on to find the articles in hard copy. You might get up from the computer and move to another machine to read the articles on film or fiche. You may stay at the same computer to read the article on another compact disk. Or, you may have to rush away with your citations to another library that has the periodical titles you need.

Some CD-ROM periodical indexes don't have abstracts, but even then the keyword search is usually done on more than just the title. The keyword may also be found in the subject headings attached to the citation. If you want, the keyword or keywords you enter may even include the name of the magazine.

Besides magazine articles, most CD-ROM systems offer extras, designed to be attractive to subscribers. In addition to keyword searching, a system may allow you to browse through subject headings. Another may let you look through the table of contents of magazine issues, then go directly to a particular article. This last system lets a library expand its magazine collection, by virtue of the purchase of a particular indexing system.

Some CD-ROM indexes include information on companies (news releases, rankings, descriptions, etc.) helpful for job hunting. There are encyclopedias, games, dictionaries, almanacs and more on CD-ROM, but this section covers CD-ROM magazine indexing.

Computers provide another type of magazine index, the on-line computer index. Of course, CD-ROM indexes are loaded onto a computer, and may not feel very different, or the difference may not seem important to you as a library user. But a CD-ROM disk is loaded onto a computer that only accesses that particular CD-ROM index. An on-line system is loaded into the computer, by computer tapes, and usually is integrated into a system that includes the computerized catalog. Thus you can walk up to the computerized catalog and select which index you want; the book index, the magazine index, another index, or other information loaded into the system.

On-line indexes are usually found in college and university libraries, but they have begun to appear in public libraries, a trend that will expand. The nice thing about an on-line system is that the search method is similar for each index in the system. You don't need to learn new commands to switch from a book search to a magazine search. Some on-line systems also offer abstracts, but at the time this is written, these systems, useful as they are, do not go on to offer the material itself. They probably eventually will, but for now a searcher must leave the computer and take to his or her legs to find the magazine article manually, or locate it elsewhere, possibly through an interlibrary loan.

Thus far we have largely discussed general magazine indexes, like *The Readers' Guide to Periodical Literature*. They index an array of material, ranging from selected professional journals, to news magazines, women's magazines, and special interest magazines such as *Car & Driver*, *Business Week*, and *Science*. In short, material you are most likely to find in public, school and college libraries. There are also periodical indexes which reference one particular subject area in depth. These are usually found in the collections of colleges, research universities and specialized libraries.

SPECIALIZED INDEXES

Specialized indexes deal with a defined subject area, and index periodicals, journals, or academic papers in that area. As a rule these indexes are found only in academic libraries, if for no other reason than that general libraries do not carry many, or any, of the periodicals indexed.

The same applies to school libraries. Specialized indexes and the periodicals they cover are beyond the scope of a middle or high school curriculum. However, serious researchers, as well as college students, graduate students, and teachers certainly should know about these indexes. If you have the opportunity to do research in a college or university library it can serve you well to be aware of some of the specialized materials you might encounter.

There are almost as many indexes as subjects, or, at least it seems that way. The *Business Periodicals Index* indexes (surprise!) business periodicals, some of which, such as *Business Week* or *Forbes*, are available in your public library. Others are targeted to specific audiences and are less commonly found. There is, for example, *Progressive Grocer*, *Topics in Health Care Financing*, and *Journal of the American Real Estate and Urban Economics Association*. *Index Medicus* indexes medical articles and papers and is, of course, invaluable to medical practitioners and students. It is available both in hard copy (book form), and on-line. *Lexus* and *WestLaw* index legal materials. There is also the *Biological and Agricultural Index, Education Index, Art Index, The Catholic Periodical and Literature Index*, and *Applied Science and Technology Index*, to name just a few.

In addition to magazine and periodical indexes, the Good Detective should be aware of the existence of other indexes. For example, there is a *Book Review Index*, and a *Plays Index*. There is a *Biography Index* and a *Short Story Index*. There is *Granger's Index to Poetry*. These are not quite so esoteric as specialized periodical indexes, and are often in larger public and school libraries. While not periodical in-

SAMPLE SEARCH PATH II

I'm doing a report on the Hutu Tribe in Africa. I want historical and cultural information, not information about the current civil war in Rwanda. (Note: On the assumption that most magazine articles would be on the civil strife between the Hutus and Tutsis the search started with encyclopedias. The periodical searches were done last and just to confirm this assumption.)

s=subject search
k=keyword search

===

WORLD BOOK ENCYCLOPEDIA
H volume (for Hutu) yielded 0 hits. Index volume referred to B (Burundi) and R (Rwanda) volumes. The articles in these two volumes yielded minimal information.

BRITANNICA
Searched the Micropaedia under Hutu. Yielded a short article on the tribe.

COMPUTER CATALOG
s=Hutus-0 hits
k=Hutu-0 hits
s=Rwanda-4 hits
3 of which were pertinent and helpful.

THE ILLUSTRATED ENCYCLOPEDIA OF MANKIND
Searched under Hutu. Found a major article. Checked index volume. Referral to 2 other articles in the set. One is an article on the Watutsi Tribe. Some help. One is an article on Social Organisation/Systems of Domination and has 2 paragraphs on the historical roots of subjugation of the Hutu people by the Watutsis. All very helpful. Just the kind of information desired.

CD-ROM PERIODICAL INDEX
s=Hutus
13 hits on Hutu Tribe, 14 hits on Civil War, 13 hits on Minority & Ethnic Violence, 7 hits on Refugees. All hits were related to the current civil strife. 0 hits on culture of the tribe.
s=Rwanda
266 hits with 33 additional subject headings under Rwanda. All related to the current strife and political situation.
Yield: 0 hits for this report.

NATIONAL GEOGRAPHIC INDEX 1888-1988
Searched on the chance they had done an article.
Hutu-0 hits
Rwanda-referral to Ruanda.
Ruanda-1 hit, but to a 1912 article. Too old and not available.

RESULTS: 4 major hits, the one big article and 3 books. Also got 3 minor hits. Enough for the report.

dexes, these miscellaneous indexes serve a similar function by indexing subjects that appear within a larger publication, either periodical or book. These and various other indexes will help most with in-depth research in college and university libraries, and possibly also at the public library.

Abstracting services are found in college and university libraries, and the largest public libraries. They are relatives of specialized indexes, with some important differences. Like other indexes, an abstracting service may take the form of a big, multivolume set that is issued periodically. Also like indexes, they cite the original material, but their special strength is in summaries or abstracts. These services exist for a wide variety of subject areas. There are *Biological Abstracts, International Pharmaceutical Abstracts, America: History and Life, Dissertation Abstracts International* (which abstracts Ph.D. dissertations), *Masters Abstracts* (which abstracts master theses), *Physics Abstracts, Sociological Abstracts*—well, you get the idea.

How do you know if your library carries any of these or others which might be more pertinent to your subject? Most university and research libraries have computerized catalogs now (thank goodness!) so you can usually do a keyword search on your subject and the word "index" or "abstract." Computerized catalog systems differ, but most allow you to link the subject and the type of source you seek in a keyword search.

Libraries often have index tables, alcoves, or sections you can browse to get an idea of what is available. As is often the case, browsing is a comfortable but not very effective way to search. Nevertheless, though you may not find what you want, browsing might turn up some gems for another search later on. And you can always check with the reference librarian, who is likely to lead you to the most useful index or abstract for your research question. If they do not know what that is, they will know how to find out. If your librarian has to search, remember to do your best to follow the search strategy so that you understand how to do it for yourself.

There are periodical indexes for newspapers. CD-ROM newspaper indexes will be discussed in the chapter on computers, but you may find local newspaper indexes, both manual and computerized. Also, many newspapers are indexed in volumes similar to magazine indexes. Some index just one paper, similar to an encyclopedia index for one set. *The New York Times Index, The Washington Post Index, The USA Today Index, The Times Index, The Chicago Tribune Index*, as well as others, may be found. These are useful for current information and for finding names and dates. There are also composite newspaper indexes for papers published by separate companies.

EVEN MORE INDEXES

The last category of magazine indexes is a true gem for the Good Detective—small, but valuable. These are individual magazine indexes, that is, magazines that index themselves. The mass audience magazines don't usually do this, especially if they are included in *The Readers' Guide to Periodical Literature*, but many specialized magazines do. For instance, you may want information on a country, its people, and a feel for its culture. Or you may want information about mercury, how it is mined, its uses, and its effects on people. You have a hunch that you could find this in *The National Geographic Magazine*, so you go to *The National Geographic Index*. In one volume, you see if your subject is covered, without looking through 20 plus hardcover annual issues of *Readers' Guide* or doing a keyword search on a computer and sifting through numerous hits until you find the *National Geographic* entries.

Consumer Reports is another periodical that indexes itself. Whether you're looking for in-line skates, a laptop computer, or a new vacuum cleaner, this index not only tells you where to find the article you want, but also tells you the last date they evaluated the product you are interested in. This last feature is handy, since some products, like computers, change rapidly.

Keep in mind there will be no uniformity among these specialized indexes. Each magazine does it their way. *National Geographic* has a one volume index which covers a certain number of years; finding an article written after that time requires a search through the *Readers' Guide* or a CD-ROM or on-line index. *Consumer Reports* is very thoroughly indexed, and is updated with each new issue. The annual summary indexes the last year and several prior years (this seems to be changeable). Each monthly issue contains a year-to-date index.

Most self-indexing magazines are, like *National Geographic*, indexed in a single volume. Obviously, articles in issues that appeared after the publication of the index are not covered, but a general magazine index, whether hard copy, on-line, or on CD-ROM, can fill the gap. Remember that CD-ROM and on-line indexes go back only to the 1980's, and thus can't totally replace individual indexes. Also, some self-indexing magazines may not be included by the larger indexing services.

All in all, it is worthwhile for the Good Detective to keep his or her eyes open for these self-indexed items. If your library has indexes grouped in one area, take the time to browse through and see what is there. And don't be afraid to ask if there might be an index for the subject area you are interested in, or for a specific magazine. There may not be, but it never hurts to ask, and you might just hit pay dirt.

Often the computerized indexes will do fine, especially if you have a current topic, or need only current information on something like solar energy in housing designs, or current statistics on child abuse and divorce. For other subjects the information need not be current. If you have your heart set on an espalier against your garden fence, old information may be as useful as new, or maybe even more useful. *The Readers' Guide* will take you back to earlier articles but you will have to search through annual volumes for as many years as you care to search.

PATHFINDERS

Pathfinders are useful tools that are only occasionally found in libraries. A researcher frequently tries several subjects or initiates a few false starts before finding pertinent subject headings. A pathfinder basically gives you a search strategy on a subject, by taking a subject, such as gun control, abortion, hate crimes, whatever, and listing the different subject headings that particular subject may be found under in each type of source, e.g., the card catalog, periodical indexes, or encyclopedias.

There are no universal subject headings; what works once will not necessarily work again in a different forum. Encyclopedias, the card catalog, or various magazine indexes may all use different subject headings or forms of names. Often you must look for different words in different sources. Pathfinders are not very common in libraries any more, but it is worth looking at if you come upon one. Computerized keyword searching does get around some of that, but pathfinders can be especially helpful at the beginning of a search and may also give you new ideas of where to search.

BIBLIOGRAPHIES

Bibliographies must be mentioned as another of the helpful tools at your library. Librarians often make up lists, or bibliographies, of books and articles on a subject. The beauty of such lists is that they are so specific. Somebody has al-

Public Library of Des Moines

DRUG ABUSE

(including drugs in sports)

Pathfinder: a guide to information on
your topic

Topic Summary: Public attention is
focused on crack abuse and drugs in
sports. Other topics for study
include drug testing, drug traffic,
and the prevention and treatment of
drug addiction. This pathfinder gives
sources of information on these and
other drug abuse topics.

REFERENCE SOURCES

Congressional Quarterly Index for news
of government actions. Index subject:
Drugs and drug abuse.

The Encyclopedia of Drug Abuse
(R615.1 Ob6e)

Information Please Almanac (R031 In3)
Index subject: Drugs: Cocaine and crack.

The Merck Manual (R616 M537m14)
Index subject: Drug(s)—dependence.

The Patient's Guide to Medical Tests
(R616.075 P651p3) Index subject: Drug abuse.

The World Almanac (R317 W89) gives the
effects of commonly abused drugs, the
number of drug arrests, and statistics on
drug use by high school students. Index
subject: Drugs.

BOOKS

Search the computerized catalog and the
card catalog using these subject headings:

Athletes—Drug use	Drugs and youth
Crack (Drug)	Hallucinogenic drugs
Doping in sports	Heroin habit
Drug abuse	Marijuana
Drug testing	Substance abuse
Drug traffic	Youth—Drug use

Sample browsing call numbers are: 362.293,
178.8, 613.8, and 615.78.

PAMPHLETS

Check the pamphlet file using the subjects
"Drug abuse" and "Drugs."

MAGAZINE ARTICLES

Search Readers' Guide to Periodical
Literature using these subject headings:

Cocaine	Drugs and sports
Crack (Cocaine)	Drugs and youth
Drug abuse	Heroin
Drug abuse—Testing	Marijuana

Info Trac" is another index available at the
Main Library.

NEWSPAPER ARTICLES

Search one of these indexes:
The Des Moines Register Newspaper Index
(ask at the librarian's desk).

The New York Times Index (at the Main
Library).

LIBRARIAN ASSISTANCE

Ask the librarians for information about
keyword searching, The Des Moines Register
Newspaper Index, materials available on
interlibrary loan, online database
searching, or films.

COMMUNITY RESOURCES

Community Telephone Counseling - 244-1010
3:00 p.m. - 8:00 a.m. A referral and
counseling service. Sponsor: The American
Red Cross.

First Call for Help - 246-6555
A twenty-four hour information and referral
number. Sponsor: United Way of Central
Iowa.

Iowa Substance Abuse Information Center,
Cedar Rapids, IA - 1-800-247-0614
A source for pamphlets and other resources.
Sponsor: Iowa Department of Public Health.

National Council on Alcoholism and Other
Drug Dependencies - 244-2297
A source for pamphlets. The council does
short-term evaluation, counseling, and
referral.

Compiled by
Young Adult Services Staff
Public Library of Des Moines
1989

Public Library of Des Moines

BIOGRAPHY

Pathfinder: a guide to information
on your topic

> Topic Summary: Many people enjoy reading
> about the lives of real people.
> Additionally, students are often required
> to read biography or autobiography for
> class assignments. This pathfinder is
> meant to assist readers searching for
> full-length books and articles on people
> of interest to them. Brief entry
> biographical background sources such as
> Who's Who in America are not focused upon
> here.

REFERENCE SOURCES

Biography Index: a cumulative index of
biographical material in books and magazines.
(R016.92 B52)

Index to Collective Biographies for Young
Readers (R016.92 Si3913)

Through a Woman's I: an annotated
bibliography of American women's
autobiographical writings, 1946-1976.
(R016.92 Ad24t)

Other similar indexes appear in the computer
catalog under the following headings:
    Biography--Bibliography
    Autobiographies--Bibliography
and on the reference shelves under R016.92.

The following booklists include chapters or
sections on biography:

Books for You: a booklist for senior high
students. (R011 B212b or R028.5 G137b or
R028.5 Ab82b)

Outstanding Books for the College Bound
(R011 Ou8)

Your Reading: a booklist for junior high and
middle school students. (R011.62 Yo88)

Other similar booklists may be found in the
computer catalog under the headings:
    Bibliography--Best books

PAMPHLETS

Check the pamphlet file using the subjects
"Artists," "Authors," "Musicians,"
"Presidents--U.S.," and "Women."

BOOKS

Search the computerized catalog and the card
catalog using these subject headings:
    S=Last name (space) first name
    S=Biography (space--subheadings)

Also look for the subheading Biography under
subjects, occupations, countries, cities,
ethnic groups, etc. For example:
    Actors--Biography
    Africa--Biography
    Afro-American--Biography
    Artists--America--Biography
    Baseball--Biography
    Crime and Criminals--Biography
    Indians of North America--Biography
    Medicine--Biography
    Presidents--Biography

MAGAZINE ARTICLES

Search Reader's Guide to Periodical
Literature using last name, first name.

InfoTrac" is another index available at the
Main Library.

LOCAL AND REGIONAL BIOGRAPHY

For books search the card and computer
catalogs under these subject headings:
    S=Last name (space) first name
    S=Iowa--Biography
    S=Des Moines Iowa--Biography

Search The Des Moines Register Newspaper
Index (ask at the librarian's desk).

Oral History audio cassette tapes contain
interviews with Iowans about local points of
interest, business, and historical
experiences. They cover local, national,
and international events. This collection
is indexed by the names of those interviewed
and is housed at the Franklin Avenue Library
(ask at the librarian's desk).

LIBRARIAN ASSISTANCE

Ask the librarians for information about
keyword searching, materials available on
interlibrary loan, online database
searching, films or videos.

Compiled by
Young Adult Services Staff
Public Library of Des Moines
1989

ready done the leg work and found exactly what is available on the topic. The drawback is that they can only cover materials published up to the time that the bibliography is prepared. Anything pertinent published after that will not be included unless the bibliography is updated.

Chapter Six

Knock! Knock! Who's There?
Biographical Sources

You have to do a report on a poet you never heard of and he lived in England in the eighteenth century. You haven't found your poet's name *anywhere*. Okay, you check *all* of the encyclopedias. Two of them don't mention your poet at all (yes, you checked the indexes), one gives you three sentences plus the birth date followed by a question mark in parentheses, then the death date, which they seem more sure of. The last one gives the poet two short paragraphs. Not really enough information for a decent report. Now what?

It's your turn to lead your book discussion group. You've read the book and all the reviews (which you found in the library through *Book Review Index, Book Review Digest, Readers' Guide*, and the index issues of *The New York Times Book Review*) and you have a number of pertinent comments to make. You want some information about the author, some background, some indication of where the author was coming from, to lend flavor to your comments. She's too young to be in an encyclopedia, and the book jacket offers almost nothing personal. Now what?

Your teacher gave you a name. You have to write a report on this person. Period. No other information provided. You haven't found your person's name *anywhere*. He wasn't in any encyclopedias and you searched back 15 years in the magazine indexes. Not a whisper. You don't even know if he's living or dead. Now what?

You went to the movies last night and have *found* your true love! Now you would like to find out something *about* your true love. You find three biographies, 12 magazine articles, and four newspaper articles on your new-found love. Could there—should there possibly be more?

You're applying for a job with Congressman Whoozits tomorrow morning. It might be a good idea to find out something about his background before the interview. You find the congressman in several magazine articles, but the contents focus mostly on his politics. You were hoping for something more up-close and personal, some background on how he got to where he is.

Yes, Virginia, not only is there a Santa Claus, there is a good chance you will find some biographical materials on him at your local library. In fact, there is a *ton* of biographical information being published. Again, as with everything else, some libraries have more and some have less.

Now is the time to apply some of our sleuth strategies. Of course, my first move would be to search the card catalog just on the chance that the person I am looking for is famous enough to rate a full-blown biography of his or her own, even if *I* never heard of him. I would do a subject search and, if that failed, try a keyword search both on the full name and just the last name. The reason for the double keyword search is that you cannot always be sure of the construction of a name. Some cultures may have multiple elements to the surname and it is possible that your subject searches might not be done on the correct element. For example, if you do a keyword search on *John adj Smith*, you have asked the computer to search for *John* and *Smith*, but only when *John* appears *adjacent* to the word *Smith*. With this search you might miss John Laughton-Smith or John Esperanza Smith do Soto.

But all of this has more to do with strategy and that is another chapter. What we really want to know is how to find out about your favorite actor, or President Monroe, or Tycho Brahe, or Cotton Mather. You will find some of these people (including many of your favorite actors) in an encyclopedia. You will also find individual biographies on many of them in most libraries. But for some people you

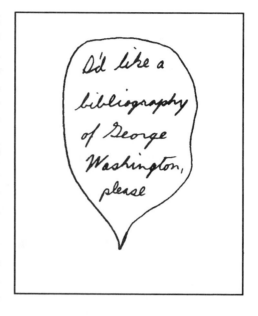

will need to look elsewhere. Fortunately, there are a lot of biographical sources being published. Some libraries have a lot, some just a few. There are sources on living people and sources on deceased people. Some sources are for specific groups of people, such as African Americans or scientists.

Now let's get a taste of some of the most likely biographical sources to be found in a public or school library. For living people you have sources such as *Who's Who in America*. This is good for basic information. It will give the person's occupation (judge, artist, physicist, etc.), date and place of birth, parents, education, positions held and dates, and address. There are other *Who's Who* books, including some *Who Was Who* titles. Some may give slightly different information, but for the most part the information in these sources will be very brief with virtually no personal background information. Just to give you the flavor of some of these titles here are a few:

Who's Who Among Black Americans
Who's Who in American Art
Who's Who in Science Fiction
Who's Who in the Major Leagues
Who's Who of American Women
Who's Who in American Politics

Current Biography is another source many libraries carry. It has biographies of living leaders in fields and professions throughout the world. These are detailed biographies that may be four to six pages long. *Current Biography* is a monthly periodical, but the annual bound volume is where researchers start. *Current Biography* has been around more than 50 years so it is a very useful source, especially if your library carries a lot of the back years. The annual volume at the end of each decade has an index that covers that decade. Each volume within the decade has an index that covers the decade through that volume, but then at the beginning of the next decade the indexing starts over. There is also a single index volume that covers 1940–1985. Why are we talking so much about how it is indexed? Because the index is the map through the maze. If you look in the index of a source you are more likely to find what you want.

While *Current Biography* covers people from all around the world, some sources are specific to one nation, culture, or ethnic group. *The Dictionary of National Biography* and *The Dictionary of American Biography* are two examples. They are both huge. They look like encyclopedia sets and are very good sources of biographical information for people who made contributions of one sort or another to their respective countries. *The Dictionary of National Biography* contains biographies of people who made notable contributions to Great Britain. *The Dictionary of American Biography* contains information on people from all sorts of backgrounds who were a factor in American history, including non-Americans, such as Tadeusz Kosciuszko, Revolutionary War hero and Polish patriot. Both these reference sources consist of an original set and several supplemental volumes.

There are collective biographies that cover a specific ethnic group or nationality. *The Dictionary of American Negro Biography* and *Notable Black American Women* contain biographical sketches of African Americans, as does *The African American Encyclopedia.* While

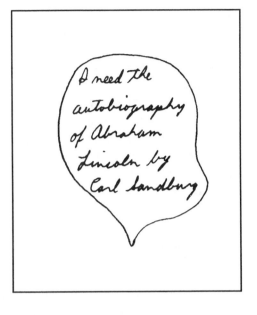

this last encyclopedia is not specifically a biographical source, it does have a substantial amount of biographical material in it. There are collective biographies of Native Americans, Hispanic Americans, American Jews, and other groups as well.

There are collective biographies based on what people do, or have done. *The Dictionary of Scientific Biography* is an encyclopedic, multivolume set designed to give the history of science through the biographies of scientists. These articles focus on the professional lives and accomplishments of the scientists covered.

Contemporary Authors and its sister series, *Contemporary Authors New Revised Series*, and others, contain biographical and professional information about current (that is, contemporary) authors. These articles include such information as titles the author has written, pseudonyms used, as well as some personal information. If you have a favorite author, but can't tell what book belongs where in a series, *Contemporary Authors Permanent Series* will help you. *Something*

About the Author (SATA) is another sister set to *Contemporary Authors* that specifically covers authors and illustrators of books for young people.

Something About the Author has a unique feature that is not exactly biographical. If you remember the name of the hero, but not the title of your favorite children's book, and you are eager to read it to your child (grandchild, niece, whatever), SATA includes a character index in some, but not all, of its volumes. Because all these sources are from the same publisher they have a common index. This can be very handy, though most libraries do not have all the various sets.

Many of the sources that I've mentioned so far have been big encyclopedic sets with lots (and lots) of volumes. There are many collective biographies in only one or two (or three or four) volumes. Some are reference books and some are books you can check out. The catalog area for collective biographies has been the 920's in the Dewey System. There, in both reference and the regular collection, you can find books on first ladies, presidents, saints, scientists, inventors, poets, queens and kings, pioneers, outstanding lives, makers of the modern world, great leaders, and so on. Increasingly, many of the newer collective biographies are being put into a subject number, such as *collective biographies of presidents* which are now cataloged in the 973's.

Some sources focus on the professional lives of their subjects and others emphasize the personal. *Facts About the Presidents*, for instance, includes personal information, but really focuses on professional activities in the office of president. Some specialized sources include comparative information for their subjects. *Facts About the Presidents* compares the ages of the various presidents when they took office, which presidents were elected without a majority of the popular vote, who had how many electoral votes, and so on. These summaries are separate from the individual biographical sketches. While you are detecting, do some exploring as well. Some of these sources offer much more than the basic information, but if you don't seek you will never find.

In most public and school libraries that use the Dewey system, biographies have been removed from the regular numbering system and shelved alphabetically by the name of the person they are about. Though cataloging trends, like fashion, do change, this is rather standard. Theoretically, therefore, it would be possible to look in the biographies and in the 920's (the collective biographies) to see if there is a book or portion of a book about your person. In reality, that doesn't always work. Apart from the fact that some books are checked out, some biographies aren't cataloged to be shelved with the biographies. As mentioned before, strictly following current cataloging rules, biographies and collective biographies would be cataloged with other books on that subject. Even libraries that set up a separate biography section may choose to put certain groups of people in their subject area rather than in the biography section. So great sports heroes may be in the biographies or they may be in the 796's with their particular sport. Musicians, classical and popular, composers and performers, might be in the biographies or they might be in the 780's. Actors and actresses might be in the 792's with the other books on movies and the theater. Business people might be in the 330's. World explorers, discoverers of new lands, and also pirates might show up in the 910's. Different libraries may choose to stack all biographies into their own section, or they may follow the rules completely, and shelve biographies in their subject areas strictly by the Dewey number. Or, they may choose to blend the two systems.

The point of all this (again) is that while browsing the shelves can be fun, relaxing, entertaining, and yield occasional gems, it is not the first research tool to use. Maybe the third, or forth. Or fifth, or sixth. The card or computerized catalog is really the index for finding these books.

What if you want to know about yourself rather than someone else? Your library might help you with this type of search as well. Would you like to know what your name means? There are books which will tell you what your first name means and how popular it is and which famous people also had that name. There are also books telling where surnames (last names) come from and what they originally meant. For example, Cartwright may come from an ancestor who made carts in early England. If your last name is Boyd, perhaps your ancestors used to live along the Boyd River in England.

The library can also help you find out more specifically where you came from. Genealogy, the field of knowledge that helps you trace your family tree, can be a hobby, a duty, or a passion. Libraries have two types of materials that can help you. First, there are books on how to trace your family history. These tell you how: how to start, how to set up a family chart, what steps to take. They explain how to find and use the resources available to search, including census materials, military records, birth and death information and so on. These books can be very helpful to the beginning genealogist. Similar books for more advanced research detail genealogical sources in the country and throughout the world.

The second group of materials that may be in your library or another library includes books on specific families, the bibliographies of genealogies owned by the Library of Congress, and local newspaper holdings that may include obituaries or other articles on family members. There are books on specific groups, like clans and tartans of Scotland, heraldry of Great Britain, German family names. There are county and state histories with information on the people who settled the area, and so on. As with everything else, different libraries will have different amounts of genealogical material. For the serious genealogist, there are whole libraries devoted to genealogical research. Many are under the auspices of the local genealogical society. Others may be maintained by a specific group, such as the Church of Jesus Christ of Latter Day Saints. Most genealogical libraries welcome researchers, though they may have restricted hours since they are often staffed by volunteers. Materials in your public library are likely to give you a good start, and perhaps point you to more specialized genealogical libraries or other sources in your area.

Your library probably also has books on different ethnic groups, religious groups, tribes and cultures. Some trace the history of different ethnic groups, including African-Americans, German-Americans, Hispanic-Americans, Chinese-Americans, etc., as they became integrated into mainstream culture. Others cover a group's culture in its original location. There are books on Native American tribes, African countries and cultures, and books on other countries, their history and culture. A good example is an encyclopedia set called *The Illustrated Encyclopedia of Mankind.* The basic set is alphabetical by tribe or ethnic group. The index lists countries and those tribes or ethnic groups who live within the boundaries of these countries, and other subjects. With that information, you can go to the article on a given tribe to find out all about them. This set also includes overviews of broad topics such as *Art and Man,* or the effects of contacts between one culture and another.

This type of research, like the rest of library research, requires that you find a point of entry and then keep digging. Every library will have different holdings, but small or large, the one you are in may harbor the gem you want to find.

Chapter Seven

What the Government Has to Say
About That!
Government Documents

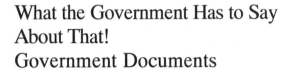

W hat does the federal government have to say?
Lots!
And lots more!

The federal government produces a huge volume of information each year. It is probably the most prodigious publisher in the country. In 1992 the office of the Superintendent of Documents distributed approximately 125.5 *million* copies of government documents. And not everything the government publishes comes out of that office.

The federal government produces transcripts of Congress (The Congressional Record) for those who want to find out just what their congress member did with his or her time last year. It publishes laws, and statistics ranging from appropriations and budgets to census data and crime statistics on to the end of the alphabet. There are reports, rules and regulations, recommendations, and findings from many scientific studies. The government produces information verging from the most practical all the way to the most academic. Literally volumes of it. Also tax forms. Lots of them.

Besides United States government documents, there are the documents of other governmental entities and of foreign countries. The United Nations with its assorted agencies, branches, and umbrella groups publishes documents. Other national governments, such as Canada, Mexico, Great Britain, and countries all over the world also produce and publish information. Individual states produce documents relating to their own economy, society, and statistics. These include individual state handbooks covering state officials and agencies, and often some historical information. States publish their own laws, state of the state type information, and so on. Libraries within a state may carry that state's publications, but often do not have many documents published by other states. For the most part this chapter will address United States government documents. A Good Detective can then seek out other documents as he or she wishes.

Most government documents owned by public and school libraries are cataloged by subject and are indistinguishable from other books or pamphlets in the collection.

Even the most commonly used government documents tend to be cataloged and treated just like any other book in a public library. People use them without necessarily realizing that they are government documents. Many are reference sources, such as *The Statistical Abstract of the United States*, an excellent source for students to get statistical information for reports and papers. Other people use this source to set up profiles for research or business. It contains statistics on crime rates, birth rates, marriages and divorces, education, death rates, accidents and many other topics. The information may be broken down by state, by region, by sex, by age, by income bracket, and so on.

Another frequently used government document is *The United States Government Manual*. This gives concise summaries of all the agencies and branches of the United States government, complete with names and addresses.

The Occupational Outlook Handbook describes a wide variety of jobs, their educational and/or experience requirements, and salary ranges. It forecasts how many people will be needed in these occupations in the future.

While students follow a wide variety of tracks to accommodate class assignments, much of the information other people look for in government documents is of a very practical nature. Farmers look to government documents for information on how to build things, on honey production, forestry products, grain storage, spring flowering bulbs, climatological data, livestock information, irrigation techniques and so on. People in all sorts of businesses want information on regulations, population and business patterns, government contracts they might bid on and more. Since government documents are cataloged and put into the collection with all the other books, the search procedure is the usual one: use the card catalog or the computerized catalog.

What other kinds of things do government documents tell you? Well, if you want to visit a foreign country, *The CIA World Factbook* gives you information about that country. If you or your library are on-line and have access to the Internet, the advisory section will keep you up-to-date on whether it is considered safe for American tourists. Did you always want to build your own rammed earth home? There is a government document that will tell you how. Is it tax time? Alas, all of those tax forms also come from the government, as well as a wealth of publications to help you figure your taxes.

There are indexes and abstracts to help you find statistics, energy research, economic indicators, and technical information. *The Federal Register* provides business people and others with the latest regulations. Other publications deal with available grant money and how to qualify for it. In short, government documents are practically a library unto themselves. And in libraries filled exclusively with government documents, such as designated depository libraries, they indeed are a library unto themselves.

In school and public libraries, government documents are cataloged with a Dewey Decimal or an LC number, and shelved accordingly. Libraries that consist mainly of government document collections use the Superintendent of Documents (SuDocs) classification number, and shelve the material accordingly. Unlike Dewey and LC, the SuDocs system is not grouped by subject matter, but it is based on what government agency issued the item. A SuDocs number will look like this: A 1.38:1190. This is the number for a 1971 single sheet publication put out by the Agriculture Department that gives the layout for a four bedroom, one-and-a-half story frame house. Another example is NAS 1.60:3367. This is for *Vibrational Relaxation In Hypersonic Flow Fields*, issued by the National Aeronautics and Space Administration.

The wide-ranging scope and variety of government publications may be clear from the above examples. When you deal with SuDoc numbered publications, you can look things up and find the number yourself, but you probably need the librarian's help to retrieve the actual document. In fact, in many libraries you are not allowed to get it yourself.

So how do you find this number? There are several ways. The government itself indexes what it puts out. *The Monthly Catalog of United States Government Publication* lists government publications by author, title, subject, series, stock number, and title keyword among others. This is published monthly with annual cumulations (a yearbook covering what was in the last twelve month's issues). There are also some special cumulations such as a subject cumulation covering several years. Another publication by the government is *The Publications Reference File*, or the *PRF*, which comes out on microfiche every two months, with weekly updates. It is the *Books in Print* of government documents. It does not list anything not currently in print. Publications are listed by stock number, by SuDoc number, by subject, title, and keyword. There are also some CD-ROM indexing systems put out by private companies. As with all computerized indexing systems, these are especially good for their keyword search capabilities.

Government documents come out in a variety of forms. There are books, pamphlets, single sheets, magazines, microfilm or microfiche, and increasingly, CD-ROM and on-line documents. Many people are intimidated by government documents, but though these sources have their own indexes and sometimes their own numbering system, a sleuth's strategies are the same. There is a wealth of information here. To reach it, clarify what you want and start working through the indexes. Ask the librarians to help you learn your way around. They will be happy to help.

Chapter Eight

Sleuth Strategies:
Five Research Methods

By now you know about the tools in the library, encyclopedias, indexes, gazetteers, and so on. The next crucial step is to think about *how* to search, how to approach a search, the different strategies to use, and when to use them. You already used research strategies when you followed information tracks through the different sources we have covered. Now it is time to improve your odds for success by discussing research methods.

Not all libraries have all the tools mentioned in this book. Some may have completely different tools. Someday libraries will use future tools that are being developed even as this is written, and therefore are not covered here. The essential thing for the Good Detective is to know how to follow a track, no matter where or how well endowed your current library is.

Some libraries don't have much money. They strive to provide their patrons with pleasure reading and can offer only minimal reference materials. In that situation, you may need to go elsewhere to research that heavy duty term paper or figure out how to rig a wind powered generator for your ranch buildings. Even the best sleuth can't find what isn't there. But be sure you understand any links your library may have with larger resources.

Other libraries, like college and university libraries and the bigger public libraries, have a bewildering number and diversity of sources. Academic libraries, in particular, try to be on the cutting edge of information retrieval systems. Here, the task is to negotiate your way through all of their materials. This book, however, is not intended to deal with those libraries except in passing.

We will look at four distinct search strategies, and a fifth default strategy. Sometimes you will use one, sometimes another. Eventually you will probably use them all. The one you start with or use at any given time will not be based on whim or the flip of a coin. It will be decided by the type of information you want and the tools available to you.

STRATEGY #1—*PINPOINT* OR *NARROW FOCUS*

The first thing to do upon starting a search is look for what you really want. While this sounds obvious, logical, and easy, most people do not do this. They are of the same ilk as the young man who went to a library and asked for sports books. No surprise, he found hundreds of sports books, and upon being questioned, he stated that he really wanted baseball books. Faced with the multitude of baseball books, he explained that he really wanted a book on a particular player, Harmon Killibrew. After he looked up that specific name he walked into the book stacks and found exactly what he wanted, but his search would have been speedier and less frustrating if he had looked for what he *really* wanted at the beginning, not the third time around.

Another example is the person who wanted books on Africa, but when he found them they didn't seem to have the information he wanted. He then looked for materials on African tribes which he said was what he really needed. But he kept shaking his head, and finally, he asked a librarian for help. As she questioned him he explained that he *really* wanted to know which tribes live in Nigeria. A quick look at an encyclopedia answered that question and he then was able to look for information on those specific tribes. (Springboards!) Sources other than a basic encyclopedia could have answered his question, but the point of these examples, and the point of the first strategy, is to decide what it is you really are looking for and look for that exact thing.

People sometimes go through mental gymnastics trying to psych out what to look for. They try *health* as a subject heading when they want books on arthritis, or cookbooks when they want to know how to cook for diabetics or for people on low cholesterol diets. They look up *animals* when they want a book on gorillas. They look up *history* when they want a book on the Civil War, or *the Civil War* when they want information on how people dressed during that time period. *Don't do it!*

Your first strategy should be to *pinpoint*. Don't confuse or sidetrack yourself with a lot of unnecessary words or thoughts. You don't have to sit down and meditate for an hour. You really already know what you want. With a minute of thought before you begin your search you can clarify what to look for. If you go to a librarian and ask a reference question, the first thing the librarian may do is question you, to make sure that what you say is what you want. You can do that for yourself in far less time.

Next, start looking for what you want. If you don't find it in the card catalog or the computerized catalog (don't forget to use the keyword search as well as the subject search), then try encyclopedias, magazine indexes, or whatever basic sources would be appropriate as far as you can determine. Usually, but not always, you'll pick up something in one of these. They are your springboards.

STRATEGY #2—*THE WIDE ANGLE LENS*

When *pinpoint* doesn't work, go on to the *wide angle lens,* which at first looks like an absolute contradiction of Strategy #1. In fact, Strategy #2 is not so much a contradiction

SAMPLE SEARCH PATH III

I am on a debate team and the topic we are doing now is gun control. My team is arguing against it. Do you have anything to support my side of it?

s=subject search
k=keyword search

===

COMPUTER CATALOG
s=Gun Control
31 hits.
In addition the librarian remembered a book about women and armed self-defense. Couldn't remember the author or title.
k=Women and Firearms-0 hits.
k=Women and Guns-0 hits. k=Women and Armed-12 hits one of which was the desired book Armed and female by Paxton Quigley.
The librarian also remembered a new book by the head of the NRA, LaPierre. Author search brought up Guns, crime and freedom by Wayne LaPierre.

Yield: 4 solid hits including 2

books that gave both pro and con.

CD-ROM PERIODICAL INDEX
s=gun control-0
k=gun control-198
The keyword search not only pulled up hits, it also listed them in order from most current to oldest which was the most useful for this topic. Several of these hits were pertinent for his side of the debate.

READERS' GUIDE
s=gun control-29 hits.
Sample search was done in the 1993 volume. Patron searched other volumes on his own. Some overlap with the CD-ROM index.

GOVERNMENT DOCUMENTS
Searched a CD-ROM index that covered 15 years up through 1992.
k=Gun Control-24 hits.
Some of these hits were congressional debates. Three good hits.

IN ADDITION the librarian was able to suggest that he find some copies of the NRA magazine "The American Rifleman" and to contact the NRA itself if he had time before the debate. The address was found in The Encyclopedia of Associations.

RESULTS: The search found several pertinent articles and books. In addition, there were avenues the patron could pursue on his own outside of the library if he so desired.

as a continuation. Suppose during a *pinpoint* search none of your potential springboards (the basic sources) came through with information that led you forward. You must then go on to other sources that are both broader and more specialized. By broader I mean tools that, for example, are not just on a single tribe, like the Hutus, but on the whole country, in this case Rwanda, and yield information on the particular group of people. Or you may have to look in books on East Africa or even the broader subject of Africa. And, yes, this is exactly like looking under *health* to find books on arthritis. The reason you started with *pinpoint* searching is that these *wide angle lens* tools will not just talk about the Hutus, but will cover a lot of subjects, hopefully including information on this tribe. It may expand your focus to see how this tribe affects and is affected by other elements in Rwanda and the rest of Africa. On the other hand the *wide angle lens* may be the only way to get at some very specific information.

Perhaps you would like to know how to tie a particularly esoteric knot. Maybe you would really like to be able to tie an *inverted truncated pyramid knot*. What can you do when you can't find that knot in the card catalog? Well, you could widen your search to look for a book on knotting, but if your library doesn't have one or if they are all checked out, you need to widen your search even further, to the most promising related topics. You might search in books on macrame and sailing and boy scouts, all of which could include information on knots. This is a classic example of a *wide angle lens*. Often you will have to look in many sources to get enough information for a really good report, or enough information to build your own electric car. It is time consuming, but a side benefit of the *wide angle lens* is that you have a chance to come across some really neat and helpful information that you might not have found in the narrower, more focused sources that you started with on your *pinpoint* search.

A second instance where you might resort to the *wide angle lens* may not seem so "wide" at first. This is when

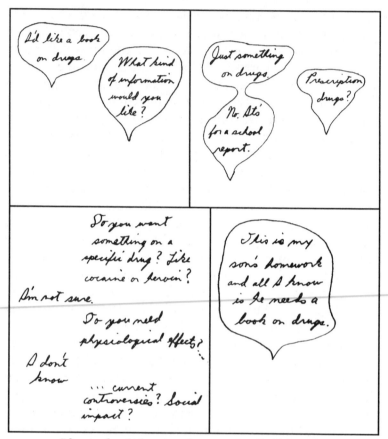

***If you don't know what you're looking for
you probably won't find it.***

your subject is very technical. Medical terms and legal
terms, for example, are often not included in regular dictionaries or encyclopedias. You may not find any books on
seborrheic dermatitis, or pityriasis rosea in the card catalog.
If something isn't relatively widespread (no pun intended)
or well known and currently in the news, it is possible you
will not find books on it. There are books on pregnancy,
strokes, arthritis, AIDS, cholesterol control and many other
conditions, but if there aren't any on your subject, go to a

specialized medical source. This could be a medical encyclopedia, a book on prescription drugs or whatever. These sources are both narrower (more specialized) and broader (covering more than just your pinpointed subject).

This type of search is not limited to technical searches. It is effective for many other research problems. If you have to do a report or lead a book discussion group on a particular author, and there are no biographies of that person, choose a specialized source for information on authors, such as *Contemporary Authors.*

There are a number of specialized biographical sources. For instance, for a relatively unknown British historical figure, the *Dictionary of National Biography* is the most likely place to find information. If the person is a scientist, the *Dictionary of Scientific Biography* might have just what you need.

Whatever the question, working from a *wide angle lens* will almost always be a multistep process. You will seldom be able to walk over to just one source and come away with everything you want. Of course, this is true of most research if you want to do a good job, but it is especially true for those times you use the *wide angle lens* strategy.

STRATEGY #3—*SHOTGUNNING*

This strategy is best when you have to search sources that are not on computer and therefore do not have keyword search capability. When you can use keyword searching, you think of the most significant word or words that describe what you want, then type that in. The computer or CD-ROM setup searches for that term or word no matter where it may appear in a citation. When you want to search for a subject and don't have keyword capability, and for example, you are using a card catalog or *The Readers' Guide to Periodical Literature* you have to find whatever word or words the author of that source decided to use. Subject terms are controlled vocabulary, that is, only certain words are used. An example is the yellow pages of your telephone book. Perhaps you want to learn the Japanese martial art of Aikido. You look it up to see if there is a club or school in town. Nothing. But the very beginning of your yellow pages has a list of subjects with "see" references guiding you to the proper headings. Under *Aikido,* it says to look under *Karate and Other Martial Arts.* There you find several Tae Kwon Do schools, a Go Ju Ryu Karate club, a Judo club, a Kempo Karate club, and an Aikido club. Bingo! You call them up, find them to be helpful and friendly, and begin your studies. Soon you are throwing people around, defending yourself against multiple attackers and—Oops! I digress. We were talking about subject searches.

It is an unfortunate truth that subject words may be different from one source to another. A card catalog may use one subject term, a magazine index something different and a newspaper index still another. Worse, the subject terms may change over time. Returning to the yellow pages, martial arts may be found under *Karate and Other Martial Arts* today, but when Judo was in its heyday several years back, the heading was *Judo and Other Martial Arts.* So subject headings change with time, as people's perceptions and interests do.

That brings us to *shotgunning.* When you don't know what subject heading to look for, try a variety of terms, and just keep *shotgunning* until you either come up with the correct term, or one that refers you to the correct term. Usually this doesn't take very long and, of course, along the way the Good Detective will seek other subjects that touch upon the research subject. An example of this is a search for information on steroids. We might search under *steroids, athletes, drug use,* and *sports (drug use).* We might look up specific sports where steroid use has made the news, such as weightlifting or football. *Shotgunning* can be very helpful in opening us up to more information and new perspectives. It's like fishing with a net instead of a hook and line. Properly applied, it can be extremely helpful.

STRATEGY #4—*SPRINGBOARDS! OR VINE TO VINE*

We have touched on this fourth strategy in the preceding strategies and elsewhere, but this methods deserves its own name. Seen any old Tarzan movies lately? I'm talking about the *old* ones that might come on late at night. In these, Tarzan gets from one place to another by swinging on a vine, grabbing the next vine and swinging along farther. People who research their family history, that is, do genealogy, swing from one ancestor to another, ideally in an unbroken line. When the Good Detective does library research he or she will often use information acquired in one segment of research to boost him or her on to something else. Speaking of genealogy, you may surmise that *vine to vine* is actually a close relative, if not actually the fraternal twin, to springboarding. Often, however, *vine to vine* or springboarding may point you in several different directions rather than one smooth line from beginning to end.

There are two ways to go *vine to vine*. The first is through information you encounter as you look a subject up in a source. You may read an encyclopedia article on a subject and come upon the name of a person, a city, or a battle that influenced the course of world history. Or you may learn of an invention that changed how people thought about the world. When this happens, in addition to searching your original subject, you swing over and search the newly found topic to see how *it* affected the lives of the people you are researching. In this way you may further fill in the picture.

The second type of *vine to vine* searching involves noticing the "other" information attached to what you have found. What are those? They are all the labels, signs, and extras that are usually hooked onto the sources. Most people treat them like so much of the visual clutter that is all over our world; the advertisements, junk mail, and background music that people have trained themselves not to see or hear. As a rule the people who are most likely to pay attention to them are librarians because they are used to ferreting out information and latching onto the slightest whiff of a clue. But these tidbits are there for anybody and everybody and the Good Detective will utilize them. So what are they?

They are the "see" or "see also" references that you will find in card catalogs and computerized catalogs and in magazine indexes. They are also in encyclopedia indexes. When your article or book has a bibliography, take a look at the titles to see if any might be helpful to you. When you find an article on-line or on a CD-ROM set up, there will often be a listing of subject headings for that article. If you got there through a keyword search, a lot of irrelevant materials may come up. The listing of subject headings can guide you to the subject heading you want to track. Even when you find materials using a subject search, note the other subject headings in the individual entries. These may help you to broaden and deepen your research. And of course, note the subject headings on the catalog cards or in the computerized catalog when you find something you want. And that is *vine to vine*.

Did some of this sound familiar? I hope so. You encountered it earlier when we looked at specific sources. In library research so much of what you do is overlapping and interrelated. And that can be a real help.

STRATEGY #5—*SLOGGING*

At the beginning of the chapter I said there would be a default strategy. *Slogging* is what research boils down to after you have had little luck with the other strategies on some searches. One such search involved finding the most recent figures for deaths from starvation (a) worldwide and (b) in the United States. The librarian who did this search slogged through a number of sources including three encyclopedias, *Facts on File*, three almanacs, *The Statistical Abstract of the United States*, and a CD-ROM magazine index using the keywords *starvation, hunger, malnutrition*, and others.

Another instance might be a search for a particular recipe. Perhaps your class is studying the Caribbean Islands and your assignment is to research the foods of that area. The card catalog can get you to the cookbooks in the 641's, and even closer, to books on world cookery and Caribbean cookery, but if you only need one dessert recipe you probably will have to go through book after book to find exactly what you want.

Another scenario. You have to do a report on violence at abortion clinics. There aren't any books out yet on the subject, but you have a long list of newspaper and magazine articles. Now it's time to apply the seat of your pants to the seat of your chair and read through the accounts your research turns up until you find information to support your thesis.

Maybe *slogging* isn't the right term. There should be a better word for it since this is often the last step in uncovering The Answer. Like archaeology, this means carefully sifting through the last layers before uncovering your great discovery. This is often when you at last find the treasure that you have been searching for.

You can always ask your librarian.

Chapter Nine

The Computers Are Coming!
The Computers Are Coming!
High Tech And Low Tech In The Library

R eady or not, here they come! The computers and
their relatives are invading the sacred Territory of
the Book. Some people like it. Some people don't.
How you feel may depend on how well you can make these
new tools work for you. Nowadays schools, print shops,
malls, banks, homes, and yes, libraries have computers. They
are used in a variety of ways: for playing computerized
games as well as education; for writing papers, letters, poetry, resumes and for other word processing activities; or for
structured learning of a particular subject. They are also used
to connect to computer bulletin boards and computer magazines and networks such as the Internet. In the library they
are used for the job they do best: information retrieval.

The first shift away from a totally book-oriented library
came with microfilm and microfiche. This primarily involved photographing magazines and newspapers onto a roll
of film (microfilm), or a flat piece of film about the size of
a recipe file card (microfiche). These formats are neither as
convenient as today's computers, nor as cozy or easy to read
as a good book. It is fair to say that microfilm and microfiche put off many people from the concept of technology
in the library. Because of the tiny print, these formats have
to be read through a machine. Often the machines produce
only dim, hard-to-read copies when the user prints a page

out. On the positive side, microfilm and fiche allow a library to pack a lot more information into what space they have. Volume after volume of old newspapers and magazines take up a lot of space which could be used for the newest mysteries, some really good science fiction, or even a new video collection. You get the idea. Seriously though, microfilm or microfiche allows libraries to provide information that people want, but that could not be housed without this technique. Also, some things, like newspapers, tend to self-destruct. Your local newspaper might be preserved on film or fiche back into the last century; the actual newspapers would have long since turned yellow and crumbled into dust.

The next step that significantly changed the experience of library users came with the introduction of personal computers into libraries. The first ones were modest machines with relatively low memory capacities, programmed largely with educational games. Now, like computers everywhere, library computers are better and stronger, and libraries and library users can tackle huge tasks on computers. While you can still use a personal computer at your friendly local library to write a term paper, résumé, or letter to your girlfriend or boyfriend, computers have grown, improved and expanded immeasurably, opening new worlds of information.

One thing that has come out of the development of the personal computer is the CD-ROM drive. CD-ROM stands for *C*ompact *D*isk-*R*ead *O*nly *M*emory. The disk looks like a compact disk that you put into your stereo, but instead of music this disk is "played" on a computer. The information stored on the disk appears on your computer's monitor as words, graphics, and animation, often accompanied by words or music from the computer's speakers. On a home computer with a CD-ROM drive, the programs usually include games, structured learning programs, and maybe an encyclopedia. In libraries, many research tools are on CD-ROM. Indexes, including magazine and newspaper indexes, indexes to poetry, quotations, government documents, books in libraries in a given state or region, and many other tools may be found. Libraries may also have the actual encyclopedias, almanacs, and other reference books on CD-ROM. The major difference for the user between a CD-ROM computer and a "regular" personal computer is the fact that you cannot input information into the CD-ROM program. It is "read only." You can interact with it, give it commands, send it on searches, but you cannot change the program or the information on the disk. When you use the regular floppy disk drives in the computer, you could add to or change the program or the data.

So what other kinds of things are available on CD-ROM? All kinds of things with new titles added daily. There is a CD about environmental issues. There are atlases. There is one with maps of over 300 cities. You find the city you want, print a hard copy, and use the map. There is a CD with summaries and criticisms of literary classics. There is one about United States presidents, another on music and musical instruments. There is an interactive disk on how the government works. In fact, more and more interactive CDs are being produced as educational and training tools.

Next up are computers hooked to a mainframe. These have a lot of power behind them and are where you find the computerized "card" catalogs in the larger public and academic libraries. Even many small libraries load their card catalog onto computer, though some of these computerized catalogs may be simpler and loaded into a personal computer rather than a mainframe. Some libraries have only their computerized catalogs on these terminals. Some, especially college and university libraries, include magazine indexes, newspaper indexes, and technical periodical indexes on their PACs (Public Access Catalogs). If there is more than one type of index or catalog on a PAC, you have to select the catalog you want to use. Usually the first or second screen explains how to select the index you want. For some systems you just select the number of the menu choice you want. For example, number one may be the book catalog, and number two a magazine index. Some systems require you to type a command word. Different libraries purchase different software packages for their computers so if you go from one location to another you have to make some mental adjustments. All computers, large or small, insist that you play the game by *their* rules. Sometimes this can be frustrating for people, but once you learn the computer's rules, you can really manipulate it.

The beauty of computers is their power. With the old card catalog you look up an item by author, title, or subject. If the library has that item, and you have the correct author, title, or subject, you will find it listed. At a main library, the card catalog may reflect what is owned by the entire library system. You can find a listing even if the book is at another building. If you are at a branch or subject library (such as a science or medical library of a university), the card catalog only lists what is owned in that particular collection. In addition, it can only tell you if the library *owns* a copy of the book you want. It can't tell you if it is in or out, if there is more than one copy, or anything else about its status.

Computerized catalog systems vary, but they generally give you much more information than the card catalog ever could. Besides author, title, and subject searching, most computerized catalogs have keyword search capabilities. This is a valuable option. As we have discussed earlier, if you don't have an authorized subject term you can search for a keyword. The computer not only looks in the subject area, but also in the author and title fields for that word or words. In fact, it will look through the whole body of each appropriate catalog entry, so if that word appears only in the summary (if there is one), or in the publisher's name, a keyword search will turn it up.

Depending on the software package that your library has purchased, you may also be able to use a keyword to limit your search by format. If, for example, you only want The Beatles on compact disks or videos, you may be able to eliminate books and records from your search. Perhaps your learning style is very visual and you find it hard to learn weaving or sewing from books. With keyword you can find out if your library has instructional videos on those subjects, or audio tapes to help you meditate. You may want a gardening video so you can see how to set up hanging baskets of flowers this summer. Maybe you think a compact disk of zydeco music will help your pace on your morning jog.

Keyword searching is also helpful when you remember only part of a book's title, or only the author's first name. They may be on the tip of your tongue, but not close enough to let you look it up by author or title. You could do a keyword search on Juliet and William and, while you may come up with some things you don't want, you probably will also pull up *Romeo and Juliet* by William Shakespeare. Keyword is very handy and probably is one of the best things to come along since sliced bread. It does have some drawbacks, however. It can bring up a multitude of titles that have nothing to do with what you are interested in. For example, if you want a book on SEALS (as in United States Navy SEALS) and you type *seals* as your search word you may come up with a few hundred or more irrelevant entries. There would be books on seals (the animal); seals, medals and medallions; books by people named Seals; and, in a big library, a few books on the Navy SEALS. At this point the Good Detective will look at the first entry on SEALS and see what the actual subject heading is rather than looking through a couple hundred titles that have nothing to do with his/her real search. As it happens the actual authorized subject heading is really *United States. Navy. SEALS*. By switching your search to this subject heading you can bring up the five or ten items that really are on the desired subject. A caution: as we have discussed, over time the subject headings may change so a book published one year may have different subject headings than a book published another year on the same subject.

Another advantage of the computerized catalog over a card catalog is that it gives information about the status of each book. Checked out. Or missing. Or on order. In most systems, circulation and catalog information are connected. As soon as someone checks a book out the computerized catalog tells the next searcher that the item is no longer available. If something is missing from the shelf and cannot be located, librarians can flag it in the computer so the next person sees it has been reported missing.

With all this power, it is hard to imagine why some people still prefer the card catalog. Perhaps it is because it is not always easy to learn something new and because card catalogs have a certain presence. If you can't find what you want, you can rifle through the cards and maybe run across something that will lead you forward. It is all right there in front of you and you feel you are in control of what you see; the computer does not select for you. If you are accustomed to the card catalog and not acquainted with a computerized catalog, then the cards are familiar and comfortable, even if not always efficient. So there are tradeoffs, but computers offer the most power, precision and efficiency, at least until the next generation of searching tools comes along.

This is not to discount the card catalog. There are still plenty in existence, and they are very good tools if you know how to use them. One of the reasons for this book is to help people use whatever tools they encounter in whatever type of library they happen to be doing research in. In some libraries you will use computerized catalogs, on-line databases, CD-ROM indexes, and in other libraries you will use card catalogs, paper indexes, and all your information will be in hard copy. The same search strategies will work no matter what your library has. You simply adjust to what is available.

Libraries may also link their computers to local or national bulletin boards, freenets, or even to the Internet. Most libraries, large or small, are or plan to be on the upcoming "Information Superhighway" to one extent or another. Most larger public libraries and college and university libraries already have an Internet connection. The Internet is a worldwide network of computer networks. These networks include databases from government agencies, academic institutions, and private libraries. There is a multitude of information on the Internet, but it can be difficult to get access. It is not as straightforward as a computerized catalog or a magazine index. There is no one catalog or index that will get you what you want, and no guarantee you can connect to the source you want at any given time. Also, there is no uniform system of searching. One network may log on one way and have one set of commands, the next network may be quite different. On the other hand, the information out there is sometimes more timely and complete than any library could afford to have in-house on paper, or in book form.

What kind of things can you find on the Internet? Many college and university libraries, some public libraries, and the Library of Congress, are connected to the Internet, permitting you to see what books and other materials they have, though you cannot read those books on-line. Various government documents are available, including *The CIA World Factbook*, weather service information, business and technical information, and much more. There are discussion groups on all sorts of topics; almost any special interest you can think of. There is, in fact, much too much to cover here. There are books on the Internet, some at your local public library. They tell you all about how to get on, how to get around, what the rules are, and what you will find there.

Many libraries belong to subscription databases, another research resource. The databases are often reached through the Internet. A subscriber gains access by entering an assigned password. Such services include databases on a wide variety of subjects, at least as diverse as what is available on CD-ROM. There are biography databases, news service databases, and one that includes business publications. Several newspapers around the country maintain databases with full text articles. There are databases on environmental information, magazine indexes, a toxicological database about drugs, pesticides, poisons, and so on. There are databases of book reviews, science and technology, engineering, education, and a host of others. These subscription services generally charge fees, either per search, or by the amount of time used. Libraries have to save money, and so librarians will try to answer questions from their own collections when possible, but the Good Detective should know that these databases are available.

Obviously, not all libraries have all these sources. Just as families and individuals have to live on their incomes, libraries have to live within their budgets. Different libraries have different priorities in their spending. School libraries try to support the school curriculum, and often emphasize research tools, sometimes even more than the local public library, because they exist to teach students how to learn to think, study and do research. College and university libraries serve students and faculty with as state-of-the-art research tools as they can afford, since they must not only teach knowledge but contribute to it, and train people to go on to make contributions within their professions. Public libraries provide a balance of informational and recreational materials. That balance may tip more toward one or the other depending on a library's budget, the needs of its users, and other resources available in the area. Remember, whatever library *you* happen to be in, the Good Detective will follow every possible clue to get the information that he or she wants.

Chapter Ten

And Now For Some Rest
And Relaxation:
Can You Find Me A Good Book?

You've done your homework. You've researched how to make your car run on hydrogen and soybean oil. You looked through all the materials on stocks, bonds, and mutual funds to assure that your retirement investments are safe. You closely studied all the alternative crops you might possibly grow on your farm. You have *all* the facts and figures in the world to support your team's side of the balanced budget debate. Your term paper is done. You sifted through obscure poetry books and indexes to locate *just* the right poem for your niece's wedding.

In short, it's all done.

Now you can sit back and read a good book. The question is, how to find one. Your librarian may be one of your best sources. Or perhaps not. Most librarians read widely or are at least aware of what is being read widely. Most have a favorite area such as mysteries, science fiction, biography, or history. If there are several librarians in your library, they may complement each other in their reading taste and knowledge. So if you ask the librarian who loves the gardening about adventure or suspense stories, he or she will either know of some or know which other librarian reads a lot in that area. Even in a tiny library with only one librarian, that person can help because he or she will no doubt be aware of what the library already owns and what new books

FEMALE
SLEUTHS

INNOCENT BYSTANDERS:

Nancy Pickard - Small town New Englander Jennifer Cain is director of a philanthropic foundation, but she spends considerable time investigating missing corpses (No Body 1986) and the murders of abusive husbands (Marriage Is Murder 1987).

Charlotte MacLeod - Introduced in 1980 in The Withdrawing Room, young Beacon Hill widow Sarah Kelling uses her Braimin connections and the help

of her art-detective boyfriend to solve burglaries which turn to murder, as in The Bilbao Looking Glass (1983).

Carolyn G. Hart - Annie Laurance, owner of Death on Demand mystery bookstore, and her boyfriend, Max Darling, join forces to see that justice is done on their small island of Broward's Rock, South Carolina. Liberally sprinkled with references to past and present mystery writers, A Little Class on Murder (1989) and other titles in the series provide lighthearted and entertaining fare.

Julie Smith - Attorney Rebecca Schwartz lives and works in San Francisco and investigates a hooker's union called Coyote in Death Turns A Trick (1982) as well as a case involving San Francisco french bread in The Sourdough Wars (1984).

Amanda Cross - Murder in academia is the specialty of tenured English professor Kate Fansler. Literary references abound in titles like Death in a Tenured Position (1981) and the recent The Players Come Again (1990). Kate is occasionally assisted in her investigations by her husband, District Attorney Reed Amhearst.

AHEAD OF THEIR TIME:

Elizabeth Peters - Dauntless Victorian Englishwoman Amelia Peabody travels to the Nile with her irascible archaeologist husband Emerson. There they investigate nefarious deeds among the tombs and museums of Egypt in books like The Curse of the Pharaohs (1981) and The Mummy Case (1985). Peters also features modern-day female sleuth and brainy art historian Vicky Bliss in Street of the Five Moons (1978) and other titles.

Anne Perry - Against the background of Victorian London, well-born Charlotte Pitt and her husband, Inspector Thomas Pitt of the London police, find themselves in high-society drawing rooms as they attempt to solve murders in Paragon Walk (1981), Silence in Hanover Close (1988), and eight other works.

HOLIER (AND SMARTER) THAN THOU:

Isabelle Holland - This author of a number of suspense novels features the Reverend Claire Aldington, pastoral counselor at a fashionable Episcopal church on Manhattan's Upper East Side in A Death at St. Anselm's (1984) and A Fatal Advent (1989).

Monica Quill - Sister Mary Teresa Dempsey, known to her young subordinates as Emtec Dempsey, is one of the three remaining sisters in the Order of Martha and Mary (also known as the "M. & M.s") and does her detecting in Chicago with a Catholic flavor in Not a Blessed Thing (1981) and Sine Qua Nun (1986).

Carol Anne O'Marie - Retired San Francisco nun Sr. Mary Helen has time on her hands and crimes to solve in 1988's The Missing Madonna and two earlier works. The author herself has been in religious life for thirty years.

FOR FURTHER READING:

Victoria Nichols and **Susan Thompson's** book, Silk Stalkings: When Women Write of Murder, published in 1988, lists series characters (not necessarily women) created by women authors from 1867 to 1987. It is available for reference use at the Franklin Avenue Library.

Prepared by Deborah Kolb
Public Library of Des Moines
1991

have arrived. A small library will not be quite so compart-mentalized as a large library, and the librarian will probably have read a wide range of book reviews. Large libraries have librarians who specialize in what is called *reader's advisory service*. A substantial portion of their jobs consists of help-ing people connect with just the type of book they wish to read.

As always, when asking about a particular type of book, be as specific as possible. If there are any authors you have read that you especially liked or didn't like, tell the librar-ian, who may rattle off a list of authors who write "like" Danielle Steel, Tom Clancy, Dean Koontz, or Mary Higgins Clark. Then you can try those other authors. Any informa-tion you give beyond "I want a mystery" would help. Do you want a bright, funny mystery? Or would you rather have a police procedural? Perhaps you would prefer a hard-boiled detective story? Or one with a protagonist who knits (or cooks) while she solves the crime? How about a crime-solving librarian? Would you like it set in the present day, or would you rather have an English Victorian setting? Per-haps something set in ancient China, ancient Egypt, or Rome? All of these tastes and preferences can be accommo-dated.

In addition to offering suggestions from first-hand (read-ing) experience, librarians often have lists that they have found or have compiled themselves. These may range from the simple "if you liked this author you may also like these authors" to specific bibliographies (lists) of horror authors and titles, mysteries with female protagonists, light, funny novels, and so on. The library may have lists of award-winning books such as Newbery Awards (for children), Pulitzer Prize winners, or the National Book Award winners. They may have bibliographies of local or state authors, mi-nority authors, or recommended books for college-bound students. Librarians both collect and generate lists of books that offer a selection of materials in different genres. They may have lists of Christian fiction, Gothic romances, historical fiction set in the American West, banned books, books set in your state, and on and on and on.

Besides lists your librarians compiled or found, there are sources that list and sometimes summarize various categories of books. They may be divided by reading level and subject matter. They may cover historical novels for sixth graders or books on handicapped children for fourth grade level readers. Some reference books are for books in series, so you can pick a series and read through it. Many people like to read books that follow the same character or characters through various adventures or mysteries.

Another way to find current books you might like is to read book reviews. Your local paper and many magazines usually include book reviews. The library will no doubt have the reviewing sources that the librarians themselves use to select books for the library. (You didn't think they *read* all of those books before buying them, did you?) These sources may include *The New York Times Book Review, Library Journal, Booklist, Publishers Weekly*, and others. Sound boring? Not really. Unlike a librarian, you can just turn to reviews of science fiction, sports books, cookbooks, or whatever your interest may be, and see what is new, what is well-written, and what sounds interesting. Then check to see if the library has purchased it. If they have not, many libraries welcome suggestions from patrons for purchases of new books or will borrow the book from another library.

Another possibility is to check the library's computerized catalog if it has one. Traditionally, fiction has not been given subject headings, but computerized entries can be more complete than was possible with a manual card catalog system. If you can think of some reasonable keywords, it might be possible to do a search on those words and perhaps the word "fiction" to pull up some interesting titles. Of course, there are no guarantees that this will work on your system. It depends on how your library's system works. If you want nonfiction you could search by subject, but you might also try a keyword search which includes the word *narrative*, as in *personal narrative* if you wanted, say a true-life spy story. If you have a favorite author, it is worthwhile to regularly check if he or she has written anything new.

For that matter, you can always look in *Books in Print* to see what your author has out in case your library somehow missed a title. You can also go to the subject volumes of *Books in Print* to see what books are available on quilting, computers, wind power, or whatever you are interested in. Of course, it won't tell you about the content of the book, but sometimes you can get ideas by just looking at the titles. In addition, you might go to biographical sources on authors and find *all* of the titles your author has written. Even if they are not still in print, your library might be able to get those titles for you by borrowing from another library. This is a possibility for your research books, too, but remember that it often takes time to get materials this way. If your report is due in a week or two it probably won't help you.

So. Want to read a good book?
✓ Check the catalog.
✓ Check with the librarians.
✓ Check for a display of the newest books published.
✓ Check any bibliographies the library might have.
✓ Check the books the library might have which suggest books to read.
✓ Check the book reviews.
✓ Check your favorite author or authors.

If you are going to be a Good Detective you might as well use your sleuth skills to find a *GOOD* book to enjoy, as well as to get your homework done.

Chapter Eleven

Is That All There Is?
No!

Is that all there is?

Not quite.

What do you *do* with all this stuff you've looked up? I mean, by now you have enough information to sink a battleship. Or write a book. Or at least to fill a five-page English report. What next?

Well, you could trot right back to your nearest library and look at a few books on how to write. There are books on how to write everything from term papers to mysteries, romances, magazine articles, journals, poetry, short stories, and just about anything else you can think of. There are books on how to create plots and characters and books on grammar. There are style manuals (books that give specific directions for laying out footnotes, bibliographic entries, forms for names, and so on). If you are lucky enough to have a library which offers its own programs, you may find a program on how to write term papers or one on available reference resources and how to use them.

Libraries have lots of information, the bulk of which is in book form, but don't ignore the chance to get information (and entertainment) in other formats. You might attend a library program to learn to smock a Christmas tree ornament, or to learn how to build a model rocket, or how to tie-dye a tee shirt. Your library may have programs on how to use the library and videos you can check out as well as books and magazines. Many of these may be entertainment videos, but look them over carefully. Nonfiction or documentary videos, some may be helpful when you are gathering information on a subject. Many, though not all of these documentary videos, come from the Public Broadcasting Network's educational channels. Others are commercial programs.

There are videos and books on how to study and get the most out of school, how to weave a rug, braid hair, or do any number of things. Sometimes studying a book may be the best way to learn something. Other times watching a demonstration may be the easiest way to learn. There are computer programs to help you learn anything from typing, to history, to math, or how to work your computer. There are interactive, educational CD-ROM programs, and there are audiotapes. You can find fiction and nonfiction books on audiotape. There are audio recordings of folk tales, how to do self-hypnosis, manage stress, learn a language, meditate, and enhance your creativity. All sorts of things are waiting for you on audiotape. Sometimes hearing something may be the best way to learn.

Some things may be available only on computer, like information on computer bulletin boards, or the hard to get to, but massive quantity of information on the Internet. In time this could include books, magazines, documents, and other forms of information that someday may *only* be published on-line. Big or small, libraries are scrambling to keep up with your information needs through a variety of formats. It's up to the Good Detective to make use of those sources even if they were not mentioned in this book. (Review the search strategies!)

So. Is that all there is?

You've read the book. You had your pad and pencil beside you all the way and carefully took note of all of the titles mentioned. (You didn't?!) In any event, you are ready to go out to the nearest library and be a Good Detective. Right?

Wrong!

This is not all there is. Not even by half. We just scratched the surface. This book is a springboard. You get to be not only a Good Detective, but also a Great Adventurer. Now you can explore your own library. See what sources it has. It will have some of the sources mentioned here and it may have others not mentioned here. There are also sources and ways to get information that haven't come along yet, but which are being developed every day. Maybe these will include the Information Highway or the Universal Databank. Probably there will be some things between here and there. The only sure thing is that new technologies will be coming. Some will be good, some will be great, and some not so great, but the Good Detective will use them all to his or her best advantage, whether looking up information to write a history report or researching a project that has nothing to do with school.

Information is out there waiting for someone to make use of it. More information amasses every day as well as new ways to get to that information. The task of a library is to help you to access it. That's what a card catalog does. That's what a computerized catalog does. That's what all those indexes do. When you make use of those sources you can use the information at the end of your search to do whatever you want or need to do. You can use it to save the environment. You can use it to save the economy. You can use it to save civilization! In fact, someday *you* might be putting information into the system for other people to access through *their* library.

Addendum

Quick Tips

WHEN ENTERING FOREIGN TERRITORY, I.E., A NEW LIBRARY:

1. Get your bearings:
   a. Find the Reference Desk (also known as the Information Desk). This is where you go to ask questions.
   b. Find the Check Out Desk. This is *not* where you go to ask questions. This is where you will go to check out materials to take home.
   c. Find the card catalog or computerized catalog.
   d. Take note of the locations for the indexes, magazines, fiction, and non-fiction books. (See 2.a and 2.b)
   e. Take note of the location of the reference materials as opposed to the things which can be checked out.
2. Notice any "helps":
   a. Directories—such as "Magazines straight ahead, Oversize books second floor south."
   b. Locator maps of the library. Larger libraries may have either one large map to stand and look at or handout maps to tell you what is where. Or they may have both.
   c. Notice and use any printed helps the library may provide such as "How to use our computerized catalog" or "How to use our magazine index."

WHEN DOING RESEARCH:

1. Clarify in your own mind what it is you are really searching for.
   a. If you don't know enough about your subject or if you have not really selected a subject to work on, start by looking in a general source to give yourself a handle on the topic.
2. Once you have determined what you want to work on, start with pinpoint searching.
3. If you don't find your subject listed in your first source, continue searching in several other sources.
   a. Shotgun it.
   b. Try variations of your search terms.
   c. Try broader headings—the wide angle search.
4. Use indexes to books, encyclopedias, magazines, etc.
   a. Shotgun it.
   b. Try variations of your search terms.
   c. Try broader headings—the wide angle search.
5. USE KEYWORD SEARCHING.
6. Notice all of the "see" references or other subject listings.
7. Expect to dig for your information.
8. Learn to take notes. Printers and copiers are great and save time, but note-taking skills are invaluable.
   a. Always note your sources. Even if you don't think you will need it for a bibliography, at least take enough information so that you can find that source again.

WHEN LOOKING FOR A GOOD BOOK FOR PLEASURE READING:

1. Check the catalog.
   a. Look for your favorite author or authors in case they have a new one that you haven't seen.
   b. If you are looking for non-fiction try a subject or keyword search.

2. If you are looking for fiction, see if the library has specific genres shelved together in an area instead of all being shelved together as fiction. These genres would be things like mysteries, science fiction, westerns, romance books, and so on. These make nice browsing areas.
3. Ask the librarians.
4. Check any bibliographies the library may have, either in handout form or book form.

GOOD HUNTING!

Index